The Boxer Within

Vickie Simos

The Boxer Within

The Boxer Within
ISBN 978 1 76041 452 8
Copyright © text 2017
Cover photo: Paul Bovolos, Paul Bovolos Production

First published 2017 by
GINNINDERRA PRESS
PO Box 3461 Port Adelaide 5015
www.ginninderrapress.com.au

Contents

Six Minutes	7
1 Born in the wrong place – it might as well have been Mars	11
2 Genetics – apples don't fall far from trees	13
3 Mum – a force to be reckoned with	15
4 Dad – the storyteller	19
5 Childhood memories – being a kid is overrated	24
6 Fruit picking – not for the softie	28
7 The Riverland – anywhere but here	31
8 A little town called Barmera – into the abyss	40
9 My first nightclub – thirteen, police, toilets, best hiding spot…	43
10 Growing up in Barmera – my sister, my hero!	46
11 Teenage years, high school – being a teenager can be hard	49
12 Leaving Barmera – my prayers had been answered	52
13 Playing soccer	57
14 Why martial arts? – About a boy!	60
15 Love interests	62
16 My first job – what doesn't kill you makes you stronger	66
17 My first overseas trip – on my own	69
18 I break down – everyone ends up in a dark place…	73
19 The printing place – the higher the rise, the harder the fall	75
20 Martial arts saved my life – saving grace	79
21 How I found boxing – boxing found me	82
22 My very first fight – what was I thinking?	85
23 The fight that never happened – my poor rib!	90
24 An unorthodox instructor – do you have what it takes?	92
25 Becoming a personal trainer – the passion begins here	95
26 My second degree grading – another stripe to my belt	97

27 It's all in your head – help comes whether you like it or not	100
28 World titles Jakarta 2007 – one moment in time	105
29 Philippines 2008 – the Gathering	110
30 Making new friends – having my back!	112
31 Always the underdog, but who's complaining?…	114
32 Gold in New Zealand 2008 – remaining humble	117
33 The big trip 2008–2009 – time for some space	120
34 The highs and the blows – a glutton for punishment!	124
35 Here we go again! – October 2010	127
36 Before the fight – extract from my journal	131
37 Six minutes – that's all it takes!	136
38 It only took eleven years – amen!	140
39 Working with kids – a change of priority	143
40 When all is said and done – today	145
41 Lessons I have learnt – two steps forward, one step back	148
Thanks	150

Six Minutes

I came out guns blazing. I was firing with everything I had, just throwing punches. I couldn't tell what punches I was throwing, or how many. My aim was to make them connect. I chased her around the ring, not stopping until the round was over. I felt my punches connecting, but I wasn't sure how many there were. I did as I was told and kept moving forward while punching. I didn't want to give my opponent any excuse to attack me.

I don't remember too much of the round. It just felt like I was in a trance, almost hypnotised. The only voices I could hear were my instructor's; the rest appeared to be muddled. This was a good sign. In the past I could hear everything everyone was saying, which distracted me from the fight.

Moving forward, I managed to connect with every punch. I don't remember being tagged; in fact, it felt like I was the only one doing the hitting. The round felt short and I didn't feel too tired. I was out of breath, but easily recovered.

I felt good after the first round; I knew it was mine! The fact that I had two rounds to go didn't even enter my head. I think I was feeling a little cocky by the end of the first round. I couldn't wait to go back in and show her what I really had. In that one minute of rest, my instructor told me that now was the time to change my style and start circling her. This was something we had been working on leading up to the fight. I remember it took twelve rounds of boxing with my instructor on a Wednesday night to find my style, and this was it. Moving forward was not enough. I needed to confuse my opponent, which meant I needed to move left or right off the centre while hitting her.

It was all about timing. I had to make sure that when I was going to use it, it was going work. To be quite honest, I don't think my instructor was too fussed about whether it was going to work or not. I am pretty sure just attempting it made him happy.

I managed to pull it off, connecting her with a double right hook to the head, and then a body shot. Unfortunately it only happened the once. She began to chase me. Not that I was backing down, but her punches began to connect, whereas mine were not. It was here as she stepped back that I noticed my blood on her gloves, specks on the white parts of her gloves, clearly not hers. But you have to expect a little blood. Seeing my blood on someone else's gloves was nothing new to me. The novelty had worn off and I had become quite accustomed to it. The sight of blood doesn't bother me. Nor can you feel the hit even when you do see the blood; it becomes part of the process. Nonetheless, while you are impressed that the opponent has drawn blood, you would still like the opportunity to fight back, perhaps draw some blood yourself, or create a little pain for them. Remember, though, this is not the real me talking; it's the alter ego that resides in the gym.

At this point I could hear my instructor saying, 'Your punches are not hitting her.'

Even before my instructor told me that, my opponent and I had one point each. I knew she had the round, but I wasn't worried. I knew I still had one round to go. I was confident that I could do it, not necessarily win, but do well. The only advice my instructor gave me was to throw any punch, and not stop until the round was over.

We met in the centre of the ring to begin the third and final round, touched gloves, and began to fight. I wanted the win so much. I felt I had worked really hard and, to be quite honest, I believed I deserved it. I thought, if anyone is going down, she is.

We were throwing punches, trying to outdo each other, trying to make the other tired, and trying to make the other give up. But I wouldn't give up. Tired wasn't even in my vocabulary, and I doubt very much that it was in hers.

This time it was not one-sided. I gave, but not without receiving; it's like Christmas! Before you enter the ring you have all these illusions, or should I say delusions, of what punches and combinations you are going to throw. It soon becomes apparent that the only punches you are going to throw, jab, cross, uppercut, are straights, and if you're lucky you might actually throw more than one. Thankfully, I was not under such an illusion. My biggest issue had nothing to do with the boxing; it was all about the mind, and also my greatest enemy. But now all I wanted to do was win. I didn't really know what the punches were, as long as they were connecting. Some did, some didn't.

In the last stages of the fight, she had the upper hand and was pushing me towards the ropes. I was still hitting, but then something happened. I slipped and fell onto my knees. I wasn't sure how much time I had left, or how I got to the ground. All I knew was I had to get up and keep fighting. My instructor thought we had more time, so he was yelling to get up and get back in there. The fall did cause a slight disappointment, but it didn't last long. I quickly realised there was no reason to be disappointed. I had fought well, so, win or lose, I should be happy. As I proceeded to get up and continue to fight, the round ended. Now it was in the hands of the gods. Whatever happens, happens; *c'est la vie*.

I went back to my corner. My instructor wiped my nose, cleaned up the blood and took off the head gear. My hair all messed up, nose looking a little worse for wear, I went back to the centre of the ring.

The judges, sitting on opposite sides of the ring and holding red and blue sticks representing the fighters, had made their decision. Was it me or was it her? Did I say a little prayer? Did I what!

Seconds felt like hours. I was anxious. How could you not be? It all came down to six minutes. As my instructor always says, 'If it's gonna be, it's up to me.'

The winner is identified when the referee raises their hand. Mine was raised; clearly I was the winner. But was I? Before jumping up and down, and making my thank you speech, I thought I'd better check to see if my opponent's hand was also raised. No… Could it be possible? I'd won! No way! I was shocked, mentally exhausted and so very happy.

While the fight under normal conditions (organised by a federation not a gym like this one was) was small, the win was big. It meant I had finally put those demons to bed. I was able to showcase my skills rather than merely survive in the ring. It was also a demonstrations in determination: you can achieve anything if you just believe. As I always say, 'To believe is to succeed.'

1

Born in the wrong place – it might as well have been Mars

I always believed I was born in the wrong place. I decided this very early in life, probably while in primary school. I used to draw pictures, write stories and imagine a different life, a life of endless possibilities. The Riverland was clearly not the place I was meant to be. I wanted to do things, to be somebody and you couldn't do that there. Marriage and kids were not something I wanted back then. I had dreams and envisioned more for myself, although today it is a different story. Now I think being a parent is one of the most important jobs in the world, one I would welcome with open arms. However, back then I needed and wanted more.

Unlike some of the people I grew up with in the Riverland, my definition of success was not measured by material things. For me, success had a different definition. It meant getting out of the Riverland and I didn't care what I had to do. The main catalyst for this drive was simple: I didn't want to have to do what my parents did, to work for someone who thought they were better than us, because they had money and we didn't. Don't get me wrong: not all the people my family worked for were like that, just one in particular. Those who had the money also had the fruit blocks, and work on the fruit blocks was what we were forced to do, picking grapes or cutting apricots while dealing with the relentless heat. I can't even look at an apricot these days without feeling nauseous. I swore I would never do that again! Not that I looked down on it, because sometimes you just don't have a choice, as it was for my parents.

I used to hear them get up before dawn, trying to be quiet so they didn't wake us, Mum making sandwiches for lunch and preparing a large flask of Greek coffee for the morning and afternoon break then returning home just before sunset to have a shower, wash their clothes, prepare dinner and do it all again the next day.

While it was very hard work and also brain-numbing, there were some fun times. When end of season came around, it also meant silly season. We would throw ripe apricots at each other and they'd stick on your clothes like glue. The stench was unbelievable, but it didn't matter; we got to forget about the hard work for a while. Despite those occasional days of fun, it was not what my parents envisioned for themselves. But when you have three mouths to feed and don't speak the language, sometimes the choices are made for you.

My sister told me that Mum wanted to be some kind of carer, like a nurse or something similar. There was also mention of a lawyer, a better suited profession, I would've thought, an advocate for the underdog. It's ironic, because what my mother didn't achieve as a career, I have achieved, not as a lawyer, but in professions where I help others. She also told me that Dad wanted to be either a history lecturer or a doctor. Given the amount of talking he does, he would've been a natural. Standing up in a lecture theatre full of curious minds, soaking up everything he said, it would have been a dream come true. And there's no doubt in my mind that they would've succeeded. It's unfortunate that their aspirations never came to fruition, and now the only aspiration they have is for their children. Find a Greek partner, get married, procreate, and of course be happy, is every Greek parent's dream. One of us fulfilled that dream; my brother is married and has a daughter and son.

That was their definition of happiness, and while to some degree I understood where they were coming from, it wasn't my definition and that's what they didn't understand. Of course I want all that for myself and more, but happiness starts from the inside and I just wasn't there yet.

2

Genetics – apples don't fall far from trees

Both my parents come from small villages in Korinthos. My dad is from Katakali and my mum is from Athekia. Despite growing up in similar surroundings, their upbringings couldn't have been more different.

My mum had two supportive parents. My pappou (grandpa) was tall and skinny, a quiet gentle soul, who never used to say too much but was a great storyteller. That's the only real memory I have of him. My yiayia (grandma), on the other hand, was short and round and had a lot to say, never held back, a gene I may have acquired and developed over the years – as the Greek saying goes, *Onoma ke prama*, which means you are the same as your namesake. Anyway, while they didn't have the money to send their children to school, they still wanted their children to do something, to be something.

It was significantly different from my father's upbringing, which was much less supportive. His mother died at a young age and his father just didn't know how to cope.

I didn't know my grandma, Mum's mum, all that well, but from the stories I have heard, we had a lot of similarities. She was a very hard woman. For example, she used to carry a cane because of a broken leg, a leg which she chose not to fix until long after it had been broken.

My first memory of her was from 1979 when I was five years old. Her whole demeanour was scary, from her limp to the way she looked at you. She didn't just look at you, she looked straight through you; well, that's what it felt like to me, but I was only five, and then twelve, which was really the last time I saw her.

She had six children, three boys and three girls; my mum was somewhere in the middle. They were the children I knew of, but there were others, some lost through miscarriage, and others through being stillborn. One, a girl, died at the age of seven through sickness.

One of the many stories I heard about my grandma was that she had a softer spot for her sons than for her daughters. Now while this sounds very harsh, I have a theory. I actually think she believed her daughters had stronger wills than her sons. Also, if genetics are anything to go by, it seems the apples didn't fall far from the tree. I found out that when my grandma's leg was finally fixed, it was not by a doctor, but by her friend who, believe it or not, was a farmer/vet. Having fixed many broken limbs on his cattle, it wasn't a far stretch to fix the broken leg of an elderly lady. Just as he did with the broken limbs of his cows, he put two planks of wood on either side of her leg. This set the bones and allowed them to reattach quite accurately.

My grandma was also a bit of a clean freak. She wouldn't step outside without making sure she had clean clothes on. She'd be very careful not to get dirty. My grandfather, on the other hand, was quite the opposite. Grandma, who was half his size, would force him to have a bath and if she wasn't satisfied with his cleanliness, she would do the unthinkable.

3

Mum – a force to be reckoned with

My mum started going grey at thirty-five, coincidentally the same year she gave birth to me. I'm sure I wasn't the cause of it, contrary to popular belief; well, at least not till a few years later. She was the parent I feared most as a child, but that had nothing to do with her size. In fact, she has kept the same figure for as long as I can remember, her weight only fluctuating a couple of kilos here and there.

While measuring only five feet, she stood tall and she had dark thick hair. Mum was very active, always attending to her garden, which my dad teases her about, comparing it to the botanical gardens. These days, she still has thick hair but it is a lot greyer, and she doesn't walk as straight as I would like her to. All those years of hard work have taken their toll. Though, despite my knowledge of training that could help her with her sore back, knees, and so on, she will always know more about her ailments and fixing them than me.

She was tough, and still is. She would say what she thought, when she thought it, and I respected her for that. I learnt very quickly that my parents' relationship was, well, not like the movies. Back then, couples stayed together no matter what, and mine are still together.

One of the main reasons I used to fear my mother was because she was unpredictable, especially when she disciplined her children. I remember the first time I swore; I think I was in my early teens. I felt this rubber object hit me straight in the mouth with great speed, and discovered later that it was a thong – and not the kind you wear under your clothes. My martial arts instructor would have been proud.

I don't think I cried; it just took me by surprise. She often used random objects to discipline me; it was whatever worked at the time. I have also been hit with a mop, but that was funny more than anything else, more so because I was a lot older and stronger and, while there was determination behind the hit, there was no power. While these days it's considered a form of abuse or an unjust way to discipline a child, sometimes it's necessary; it certainly was for me and on more than one occasion. A smack on the bum or the leg never really did any harm.

These days, however, it's me who's a little taller and stronger, so putting my mum in a headlock is something she is more than used to.

My mother and I have many similarities. We both have a tough exterior but soft interior, and we are both relentless, like dogs with a bone. We can't sit still and we refuse to do something if we are pushed, as we like to do things in our own time and not on someone else's schedule. We often say what we think, despite the consequences, probably because those who know us know that it comes from our heart. On the downside, we can sometimes put people offside, but we don't really care about that, although I think subconsciously we probably do. It's also because we like to give our opinions. As my friends have pointed out, I can go on and on, and not know when to stop. My mother's a lot like this too, but it also really depends on the topic. It's more the generic stuff, unmade beds, washing not being done, and so on.

I also found out that whatever money my mother made as a teenager, she would put some away for safe keeping. She was happy to share it with her younger brother, but he told her to save it for a rainy day. I'm very much the same in that respect; as much as I spend money, I also save it just in case, and I don't mind sharing it with people.

I remember Dad telling me a story about teaching Mum how to drive. Let's just say she got out of the car and vowed never to drive again, even before he tried to actually show her. To her defence, having had him as a driving teacher myself, I could understand her frustration. He wasn't the most patient teacher.

I hate to admit it but, growing up, I never asked my mother what she wanted to be or do with her life, never asked about her chosen career or her life's aspirations. It's only now, as I'm older, that it seems so important, probably because I'm so determined to achieve my dream that it breaks my heart to know that my mum never got to achieve hers.

She has changed over the years; she has hardened, but has also softened in many respects. She's weathered disappointments, but also celebrated achievements, including her grandchildren. She has had numerous falls and dislocated her arm, but still remains active. She has many lines on her face, outlining some of life's hardships, around her eyes, her mouth, like a road map.

Among the many things I am proud of and thankful for is the way she stands up for her children. I'm very much the same when it comes to my friends, friends' kids, and family. No doubt I would be the same with my own children. One of my most memorable moments was when my aunty (Mum's oldest sister) was visiting and she told my mother that she saw me smoking down by the lake. I was listening at the time, because my room and the kitchen were only separated by a paper-thin wall. Anyway, there I was thinking, 'Shit, she's going to kill me.' But I had nothing to fear; my mother's response was 'You look after your children and I'll look after mine.' That says it all about my mother. I guess you could say that she was one of my first female influences.

My mum grew up during World War II. She is a woman of little detail in what she says and how she says it. When telling a story, she would never bore you with details – you know, those important elements that make a story. No, the trick was you had to know exactly what she was talking about and fill in the details yourself. Watch out if you didn't get it the first time. Better than that, three hours after she tells you a story, she'll bring up something random about the story and expect you to know the answer, and watch out if you don't.

Growing up, my mum says she never fought with her siblings – hard to believe, but her brother in Greece confirms that it was true. She hated conflict and tried to stay away from it as much as she could.

If she was screamed at, she would cry. She remembers only one time when she was involved in a fight with her sister, and that ended up with Mum getting a kick up the bum.

Grandma sent my mum and her sisters out to work. Grandma was ahead of her time. They were teenagers at the time, around fifteen years old. Although it was normal for poorer families to send their children to work, and at a much younger age, it wasn't as necessary, but Grandma felt that her daughters needed to learn a trade. She wanted all her children to be able to support themselves. Like all the siblings, Mum gave her money to the family.

I've said it before and I'll say it again, my mum was like a dog with a bone, relentless in her actions. For example, threading cotton into a needle or getting the sewing machine to work, she would keep at it until the damn thing did what it was supposed to. Of course, there was no patience involved, quite the opposite actually – such as swearing at the machine or, well, just swearing at the machine.

My mum seemed to enjoy hanging out with her brothers more than her sisters. She was a hard worker, so much so that she worked at a number of different labouring jobs, definitely a characteristic I also picked up from her.

She went to school for five years, even going to night school. She really enjoyed it and even made good grades, but that's as far as she went. The reason was that some of teachers had to go to war, so the teaching had to be fast-tracked. One thing that I envied and envy about my mother was her ability to make friends and keep them. She is still in touch with her three childhood friends, Panagoula, Athanasia and Giannoula.

My mother came to Australia with her brother and two sisters when she was twenty-three years old for a better life. Their departure from Greece was not an easy one; her parents did not want her to go, but they knew she would have better opportunities in Australia.

4

Dad – the storyteller

When World War II ended in 1945, Dad was ten. At that time, he had a cat called Socrates. He was a lover of cats just like me. The cat used to jump up on his shoulders. He was also able to find his way home whenever he heard my dad's call, no matter how far away he was.

Dad went school to learn the alphabet, with no pencils and no paper. The teacher used to write on the dirt. Every year they went to school, it was like they were going for two; it was done so that the older kids could finish their schooling quicker. My dad's teacher was so impressed with him that he visited Grandpa to tell him so. He also told Grandpa that he should stop drinking, instead save his money and send his child to school. The irony was that my Grandpa was actually involved in agriculture, but much preferred a drink or two. Dad was devastated. He wanted to learn; he would've preferred endless days at school, where he could learn about the world, rather than jobs that required physical labour. Unfortunately, he ended up doing the latter, living to work rather than working to live.

My dad had many options. He considered entering the police force but Grandpa said, 'What do you want to do that for?' so Dad gave up on the idea. The next opportunity came via the air force, working in telecommunications. He was accepted and looking forward to going, but it wasn't meant to be; the idea was once again shut down. This time, however, it wasn't his father who opposed the idea but his mother. She had heard about all the deaths that had occurred in the same week he was accepted. He tried to explain that they had nothing to do with the job he would be employed to do, but she didn't want to listen or didn't understand. Either way, she begged him not to go, so he didn't.

Lucky for my dad there was a third time lucky; maybe the universe was determined to set his path, even if he wasn't. This time around he was accepted into the navy and nothing was going to stop him, not even his parents.

As time passed, my dad's career aspirations became more ambitious, but that's all it was – ambition. I think the lack of emotional support played a huge part in my dad not continuing with his school education. By admission unable to go to school and get an education really broke my father and I don't think he ever fully recovered. I think what he wanted most was his father's approval, but he never got it. I'm guessing, because his father probably didn't get it from his own father. My grandpa was never really supportive of his children; or rather he didn't know how to be. He told them they could do whatever they wanted but he had no real interest in what they were doing.

My dad went into the navy for two years. He was involved with telecommunications and the secret police, skills that he had to learn through a special school. The job gave him the opportunity to travel the world, something we both have in common.

Dad never owned any dress clothes but wore only his navy clothes. That was until his older brother Vasili gave him a pair of pants that he had made for himself. The family was so poor that they used to share a suit which Vasili had made. There was also a pair of shoes which were worn by most of the family members, including Pappou, Theo Pavlo, Theo Vasili and my father

Dad came to Sydney on 1 August 1961, when he was twenty-six years old. He was hoping for a better life and the navy was not willing to pay him any more than the standard. There were so many migrants on the same boat, coming to Australia, not knowing the language, having to survive on pure instinct and luck.

He would've remained in Sydney with our relatives, but they had promised the accommodation to someone else and, because he knew no one else in Sydney, he came to South Australia. After staying in Adelaide for eleven days, he travelled to the Riverland, 222 kilometres north of Adelaide. Just like in Sydney, he was told by relatives who lived there that it offered more work opportunities.

One of his first jobs was fruit picking for two weeks. He was employed to work from 8 till 5, but there was nothing to do. There was no fruit, so he had to find random jobs. For three months, Dad didn't have any work. None of his family wanted to help him unless they got something out of it. He finally found work at a the Berri Winery, where he built cement tanks, but hurt his back and, given the injury, he could no longer continue with that line of work. Instead he ended up working in labouring jobs that had less impact on his back. He worked there for two weeks, seven days a week, ten hours a day. His next job was picking apricots, working on the land, a labouring job, something he didn't want to do.

Six months after his arrival in Australia, Dad met my mother. The meeting was organised by his brother and Mum's older sister. I heard a story about when my parents first met, but as of late the story keeps changing. Anyway, the most consistent version goes something like this… In those days, women were not allowed to have an opinion; they just had to learn to be quiet, otherwise they would be 'left on the shelf'. When my father went to see his potential bride and asked for a coffee, he was very surprised by her response. She told him he should fix his own, a direction given by her eldest sister. This attitude, according to my dad, would have made her less appealing, so he claims that by marrying her, he saved her. The jury is still out on that one, as my mum has a rebuttal and claims she married Dad when it was dark, so she couldn't really see what she was getting.

My parents were married on 19 May 1962 and moved into a house provided by relatives. There were no tables, chairs, cutlery, nothing, and they slept in a bed with ripped sheets. In 1971 they moved again, this time to a picker's quarters, a one-room house designed more for a single person or couple looking for work, not a family of five, but we made it work, or should I say my parents made it work. I don't remember what the inside looked like, only through photos, but I do remember the outside was made of grey brick.. They remained there till 1977, then moved to a Housing Trust home, which according to Google is 'a not-for-profit community-based organisation to prevent homelessness by providing community housing', in the town of Barmera, where they still reside.

One of the greatest challenges faced by my parents when they first came to Australia was that they didn't speak a word of English. Back then, there were no shop displays, which is what people used to communicate. So without speaking English, without the displays, communicating was going to be a problem. For example, if they wanted to buy eggs, they would act like a chicken; asking for milk, they would imitate milking a cow. On one occasion, asking to purchase matches was a harder task than expected. You see, in Greek, the word matches is *spirta*. So when they asked for *spirta*, the guy behind the counter, who was actually Greek, thought they were looking for someone, not something.

Dad used to send clothes, video recorders, anything he thought his family in Greece might need, but they were never grateful. This angered me, because I felt he should have paid more attention to his own family, get us established first, and then worry about his family in Greece.

Mum was not as family-oriented. That doesn't mean she didn't care, but she was more a realist. She also seemed more adventurous and happy to go anywhere, be it Sydney, Melbourne, anywhere really.

Unfortunately, the Riverland is where they stayed and still reside now. I say unfortunately, because despite Dad's need to be with family, they didn't feel the same way. Some of Dad's relatives in the Riverland did not treat them well. Rather, they treated them badly, especially my mum, because she was a real hard worker and they didn't like that.

Fast forward to 2017 and my parents have not changed all that much in character. My dad still loves to talk and tell stories. He tells them with so much detail that you feel like you're there. Or you want to shoot yourself, because you've either heard it before or he hasn't reached the point of the story yet. His love of detail is also a trait that my sister shares, a trait that I like to remind her of on occasion.

My mum, on the other hand, has no time for detail, as mentioned earlier. She also answers for Dad and he answers for her, which is normal for married couples. This has become especially noticeable in recent years. She has no filter and has no problem saying what she thinks, whether she has known you five minutes or five years. She has not only done this with friends, but she has no shame in doing it to me. For example, just eleven minutes after being introduced one of my friends for the very first time, she asked her if she knew any single guys for me. While I could've killed her at the time, like a handful of others she's done this to, we know it comes from the heart. And that is what I want my friends to remember the next time I do it.

5

Childhood memories – being a kid is overrated

One of my first memories of my dad was when we used to go to the soccer together. That was the highlight of my weekend. I loved the game, the boys, and the chops and sausages that used to make your mouth water. I also used to stand behind the goalposts and chase the ball every time it went out. That was the tomboy in me, but you don't have to be a boy to like soccer. So every Sunday we would go to those games, come rain, hail or shine.

Each town had its own soccer team, but we would support ours. It was better, though, when all the towns or teams had to play in one location. That became very significant as I got older. I would go to the games more to see the good-looking boys than to see the game itself.

Any time there was a school camp, my mother never let me go, despite my tears. She was like a drill sergeant in the army, probably worse. You learnt very quickly never to argue with the woman, that once she said no, that was it. You could've tortured her, but she would have never given in. Dad would fight for me, but it was a fight he always lost, until one day she agreed to a sleepover for one night at school. I was so happy I was allowed to go, but it was short-lived. We were surrounded by a lot of land, and what I mean by that is there were a lot of places where you could cause mischief. I used to love climbing trees and playing outside, making up stories as kids do. During the sleepover, I stayed out all day and most of the night, until Dad came to take me home.

The next morning I found myself with my little finger enlarged. I had managed to get a splinter and it had become infected. Worse than that was the chest infection I caught. As I said, I used to love playing outside. It didn't matter that it was cold; playing was more important – until I got sick, that is. It was a very, very long time after that before I was allowed to go to camp, or any sleepover for that matter.

My brother taught me how to draw. I can't remember exactly how old I was, but I was young. I wasn't too bad either. I guess being accepted into the North Adelaide School of Arts twice is proof of that.

I remember he taught me how to keep to the lines of the picture, the use of different colouring techniques, and how to set up grids if you were going to draw something bigger than the original. Drawing and writing was my escape, especially when it was cold outside, and living in the country there wasn't much else to do. Mum used to always compliment the way I would stay inside the lines. My parents loved looking at my pictures and Dad used to love reading my stories, more so because Mum couldn't speak or read English, although these days she knows more then she lets on. Once she learns a word, she tries to use it in every sentence and she certainly knows how to use it in the correct context.

Playing board games and cards was something we also did, especially on the weekend, and especially when it was cold and wet. Come to think of it, we only had the one board game, Monopoly, which became my favourite and still is. At first, I was too young to understand all the rules of the game. My siblings taught me about throwing the dice and then moving around the board first and then, as I got older, I was introduced to the purchasing of houses and hotels. My siblings also taught me how to write my name, and to count, in both Greek and English, before I even started school.

My sister would've found it the hardest, being the oldest, and being a first-generation Greek kid. Everything would have been a challenge for both her and my parents. They obviously couldn't have helped her with her homework – well, unless it was Greek – and emotional support was also lacking. Growing up in a European house, you tend to speak your native language first. I can only assume my siblings did not want me to endure the same difficulty they may have had. I always used to ask my mother why she didn't have another child after me. She used to come up with ridiculous reasons to make me laugh, such as 'Oh, sorry, I should've asked you first.' So now it's become a running joke.

One game we used to play as a family was a Greek card game, called Xeri. The only problem with it was that you had to have a team of two, which meant someone in our family was always left out. Once my brother moved out, it was easier. It was always Mum and me versus my sister and my dad. We still sometimes play the game when we go to visit our folks. My mum really enjoys the game, especially when she's winning, but not so much when she's losing. She goes completely nuts, abusing the cards; it's just hilarious.

I remember when I was a child, girls got the rough end of the deal. That was especially the case when it came to housework. In my eyes, boys got more respect. In our house, the girls always did the housework. My brother was never allowed to lift a finger – it was not a boy's job to wash dishes, make his bed, or anything remotely related to housework.

I must admit I got away with it for a while, being the youngest, but that didn't last very long. My sister stepped in and I too had to help out. She used to make me do the ironing. I hated it, which is probably why I don't own any clothes that require ironing now.

The one thing I hated more than anything, even the ironing, was waking up really early on a weekend to follow my parents to work. My siblings were the same. Regardless of whether they had school or work through the week, they had to get up on the weekend and help my parents pick grapes or cut apricots. I was too young to stay home on my own, which meant I spent a lot of hours exploring someone else's property or sitting in the car. The days were long and the fact that I was not allowed to help did not impress me; even as a kid I was very opinionated. That has changed a little, the difference being that I just pick and choose my battles now.

Though my parents weren't treated badly, it was just really hard work, and I thought they didn't deserve it. In many cases, though, circumstances beyond your control force you into these situations. I guess that's why I work a multiple of jobs in three different areas, so I'll never be forced into a similar situation.

6

Fruit picking – not for the softie

My parents used to cut apricots and pick grapes, but what I remember the most is them picking grapes. Watching my parents picking grapes was not something I enjoyed doing. I hated that they had to work so hard and not make a lot of money. The good news was that at least the people they worked for were good people and family friends. That made it a bearable experience; not to mention the fact that once I was also allowed to work too, I could make some money.

The Riverland always seemed hotter than other places, especially when picking grapes. It was easier to stay cool if you wore cotton. My mum would wear long pants and a long-sleeved shirt and a cloth around her head. She also used to wear rubber gloves, the kind that you use for washing dishes. The rubber gloves prevented soreness – that is, the blisters. They also prevented any bites. You'd get the occasional red-back spider, but it was predominantly the huntsman that would frequent the vines.

There was quite a method behind picking grapes. You'd begin from one side of the vine and travel to the other side. There were also no stools to sit on. You were on hands and knees for the whole time. Speed was also very important: pick, pick, move, pick, pick, and move. The idea was to clean the vine of any grapes. I remember my mum was always quicker to finish than Dad. I think he preferred the conversation rather than the work, and who could blame him?

Grapes were in season around February, March, after the apricots died down, so it was always really hot. The weather was always around

40 degrees, stinking hot, and the smell was horrible. It's really hard to describe. Imagine leaving citrus out for hours in the sun and then smelling it. The smell was very off-putting.

Worse, however, was the smell of sulphur. You could smell it a mile away and it would follow you wherever you went. It would be in your clothes, on your hair, all over your whole body. The sulphur was used to 'cook' the apricots overnight. Then they would be laid on the grass to dry in the sun. In those days, there were no machines like there are now. So, apricot by apricot, you'd lay them on a tray, face up, taking the stone out of each one. The tray was A2 size, so it was much easier working with a partner than on your own. I worked on my own, so that was a lot harder. For every filled tray we would make around $2.50; the most I ever made was $50.

My first memory of my parents working, especially Mum, was when I was about five years old. Dad would pick me up from school and we would go straight there either to help or to pick Mum up.

The vines appeared to be never-ending, so waiting for the season to end seemed like an eternity. I think it would take about an hour to finish one side. My mum would finish her side then go to the other side and help Dad. When picking grapes, you would either lay them on a sack or put them in a bucket. The bucket was easier to fill, given its size. Whether to use a bucket or a sack was the employer's decision. It depended on how many grapes the winery required. Every time I'd go to the block to watch my parents work, there were always sacks. Imagine working twelve-hour days every day for about three months straight. That's hard work, especially with the work being so repetitive. My parents cut down on their hours of work as they got older.

Conversations with the other workers and employers alleviated the boredom. Coffee breaks were also a good distraction. You could smell the coffee from wherever you were. My parents drank Greek coffee. It was usually made in a small cup, with the thickness of the coffee left in the bottom of the cup. Mum used to read the coffee cups after everyone was done. She still does it now with a little coaxing. I was also allowed to have some; perhaps that's why I like coffee so much now. The coffee was followed by some Greek biscuits. You would dunk one into the coffee, but be quick before it fell into the cup. The breaks were not timed, but were monitored closely by the workers. My mum would usually be the one to get everyone back to work. They had a job to do. The longer they sat around, the longer the work would take to complete. Unfortunately, it was not a job that had an ending – until you heard the tractor coming to pick up the sacks. Job over till tomorrow.

Spending many years watching my parents cut apricots and pick grapes has put me off eating them. I can't stand the sight of them. Eating them reminds of the Riverland. It brings back all those memories, memories I prefer to forget.

7

The Riverland – anywhere but here

Going back to the Riverland was not something I enjoyed doing. It was purely out of obligation; my parents still live there. In fact, putting up my middle finger every time I passed the 'Welcome to the Riverland' sign became something of a tradition that even my siblings followed. But it was not the actual place that made me want to run home to Adelaide, it was certain people. Narrow-mindedness, Hicksville, backward-looking, back-stabbing, deceitfulness and gossip are all words that come to mind. In fact, some were so deluded they couldn't see the difference between reality and fantasy. They walked around with their noses up in the air, like their shit didn't stink, while at the same time keeping their own deep dark secrets – pot, kettle, black! But that was okay, as long as no one found out. Even if they did, as long you were part of the elite group, you could do as you pleased. While some of the Greek residents would want to convince the unsuspecting that it was not like that at all, they knew the truth and so did I. I had seen it with my own eyes. If you didn't fit the mould, you simply didn't fit at all. How could anyone get away from it?

I made numerous visits to the Riverland, but they became fewer and fewer as every year passed. If it wasn't for my parents, I wouldn't have gone at all. On those trips, I also made the not so surprising discovery that friendships were not made but forced. What does that mean? Basically, you didn't really have a choice because one school in the area covered two to three towns. For example, if you lived in Loveday, Barmera, Berri and Glossop, you would usually end up going to Glossop High School. Renmark had its own high school, as did Loxton. While not everyone followed this system exactly, that was generally the way it went.

The friends I had at school are all married with kids now, some happy, some not-so-happy, but to an outsider they all looked happy. That was the beauty of the place. It was almost like you lived in a parallel universe, like living the life of the *Stepford Wives* meets *Mad Men*. Pretending is what they did best and still do. It was part of the conditioning that the children got from their parents; no matter how unhappy you were, you must appear to be happy. Why? So people didn't talk about you and your dirty laundry. Ironically, everyone knew everyone's business, so you had to be pretty good at keeping a secret. I almost felt sorry for my school friends, because I knew at the time that getting married was not their first choice, but their parents' choice.

I mainly hung out with the same two girls. One wanted to be a fashion designer and the other a hairdresser. That would have required a move to the city, which was simply out of the question. That was not what the parents wanted for their children. It wasn't in their plan, and it didn't matter what their children wanted. You needed to stay, get married and procreate. That did not require a tertiary education; basic schooling was enough. This related more to the Greek females than to the Greek males, but there was the occasional male who had to make a similar sacrifice. Although this may sound like a biased point of view, given that the same thing may have happened in other cultures, it was the environment I grew up in. Generally the boys could do what they wanted, stay out late, drink, and get away with almost everything. Of course, their activities didn't include housework; that was women's work. Unfortunately for my two friends, neither got to experience their passions; instead both got married in their early twenties, like so many of the Greek girls I went to school with.

I have always been known for my dry sense of humour and sarcastic personality, not the greatest way to make friends, but I didn't care what people thought. I always said what I thought back then, and that hasn't changed all that much now. It's just that these days I'm able to resist the temptation, and choose my battles accordingly. The only time this has failed is when emotion has taken over. That's the biggest challenge, because it's in those situations where I tend to do or say the wrong thing for the right reason.

I was raised in an environment where status meant everything and circumstance meant nothing. It was imperative that nothing bad was said about you – oops! This was especially poignant for my dad, and especially when attending any kind of Greek function, but I didn't care. Just like most teenagers, I was selfish and self-absorbed, which made such functions the perfect springboard for my rebellion. I was sick and tired of status being the be all and end all, and the fact that people were measured by the size of their wallet, rather than by the kind of people they were. Greek dances were notorious for this. Halfway through the night, the committee would throw an auction to raise money for further functions. They would auction off items such as bottles of Scotch, big-screen TV sets, plants, anything and everything. While there's nothing wrong with that, what frustrated me would be the people bidding. It was the same people, with the same big wallets, with the same big mouths, throwing their money around like it was nothing.

Let me set the scene: as we entered the hall – most of the dances were held in a hall – two committee members were positioned right near the doorway. They were there to collect your money. Twenty-five to thirty dollars was usually the entrance fee, which covered food and payment for the band. Anyway, as I entered the hall with my family, all eyes were suddenly focused on us. Why, you ask? To see what we were wearing, of course. Wearing the same thing to two different events was incomprehensible, just asking for trouble, especially because all the same people attended and everyone knew everyone else. A new outfit was a necessity, whether you could afford it or not. As we made our way to find a table, I noticed the same groups sitting, eating, dancing and drinking together.

Drinking was one of my favourite things to do. Unfortunately, not so much for my father, who at the time seemed to think that he could control everything I did. He tried, but was unsuccessful. Even now he tries, but to no avail, though I think he has finally come around to understanding who I am and what I want, and that I will always be a free spirit. I loved my alcohol, especially my Scotch and lemonade. What I loved more, though, was to dance and drink, holding a glass in each hand. That used to irritate my dad no end. I thought his head would explode. But the more it irritated him, the more I did it. If I was going to be treated like a child, then I was going to act like one. Thinking about it now, it probably wasn't the smartest thing to do. What people said mattered a lot to my parents, and I should have respected that. But I was a teenager, and as I mentioned earlier, teenagers are selfish, and self-centred. Throw in a controlling parent, and it spelt chaos. However, in my defence, perhaps it was just my way of dealing with problems I never knew I had.

One of my fondest memories was when Mrs Toole's priest came to visit her. Mrs Toole was our neighbour. She lived two doors down, married and aged in her sixties. She was smart, sassy and could be very sneaky. She was like the grandma I never had. Mrs Toole and I had regular poker games on a Sunday afternoon. There were never any visitors, which is why we chose to play on that particular day.

Sunday was usually reserved for church and Sunday roasts, two things Mrs Toole never regularly did. Mrs Toole was sitting in her beige rocking chair, while I was sitting on the floor opposite her. We played with one, two and five cent pieces; this was serious stuff. While we were playing, there was a knock at the door. When Mrs Toole called out to ask who it was, Father Brian announced himself. What happened next was priceless: I couldn't believe how quickly Mrs Toole could move. I collected the cards and hid the money. 'Hide them in the kitchen,' she said. I put the table back and then opened the door. We greeted Father Brian like two guilty children who had indulged in too many sweets. He seemed none the wiser, but then we weren't entirely sure about that.

Once he left, we had a bit of a giggle about it, and resumed our game. Just because I was a child at the time didn't mean she let me win. Our relationship at the table, so to speak, was equal, and that's what I enjoyed most about it. I had no grandparents growing up, so she was the closest I had to a granny. Mrs Toole died when I was in my late teens. It was a sad and sombre moment as I remembered all the good times, and especially this particular story.

Mrs Beech or Cathy, her first name, which I still find hard to call her after all these years, was my champion. She took a real interest in me and at a recent reunion after over a decade, she exceeded all expectations. Back then she was loud, straight to the point, bent the rules for her students, made us laugh, but was no pushover, and nothing had changed. She told me the story about the day she discovered I had head lice; rather send than me off home, she was fascinated more by the lice in my hair. I also found out that she really did love the kids she taught. She was genuine, the real deal, and would always go above and beyond.

She always tried to convince my mother to let me go on school camps. 'A' for effort, but it was never going to happen. She was always on my side. Some claimed that I was the teacher's pet, and maybe I was. It was really nice to have someone take an interest, especially a schoolteacher, because the good ones were few and far between. As mentioned earlier, I was a bit of a tomboy. I had short hair and never wanted to grow it long, whereas these days I can't stand it short. I also didn't like wearing dresses and if I was forced to, which by the way was very rare, I would cry. I love them these days, though: they make me feel powerful and sexy – what a combination! Anyway, she always used to ask me, 'When am I going to see you in a dress?' I used to say never, but when I saw her recently, I couldn't resist and wore one.

However, fun as it was, I didn't spend too much time in Grade 5, because that was the year I got sick. Why did I have to get sick that particular year? Why didn't it happen while I was in high school? There were plenty of teachers and classes there I didn't like, which would have made it worth the sacrifice.

Growing up, I wasn't the strongest kid physically and I think playing outside in the cold took its toll. It started with the occasional cough, but then it got worse very quickly. The coughs turned into asthma attacks. I was consistently unwell.

My parents took me to the doctor. Our regular doctor was away, so we saw a new one. He told us it was just a cold and that I'd be okay, to go back to school.

But the symptoms didn't go away; they got worse, so my dad made another doctor's appointment. Thankfully, our regular doctor was back and his diagnosis was vastly different to that of the previous doctor. He told us that I had a combination of glandular fever and a chest infection and that if we'd left it any longer, it would've been fatal.

The recovery, I think, was worse than the sickness itself. I wasn't really eating properly and my mum always made me drink chamomile tea; even today the smell makes me feel sick. Weekly visits to the physio, with cupping and massage, were the main treatment. The massage was okay, but the cupping really hurt. I hated it! I always used to cry having it done, although I knew it was for my own good. I'm not sure how long it continued, but I do remember I missed a lot of school and it really took its toll on me physically and mentally. It makes me wonder whether it's one of the reasons why I got into fitness.

Before making my move to the city, there was someone else who made an even bigger impact than Mrs Toole or Mrs Beech – a boy. He was no ordinary boy. Patrick was my first love. He was the boy I was going to marry and make babies with – young girls and their vivid imagination! But I was only thirteen.

I met him while walking to class, and all it took was that grin to take my breath away. He had dark hair and dark brown eyes, and he had me at 'Hello.' I thought about him day and night, and any opportunity to talk to him made my day. I wanted so much to be his girlfriend, but it wasn't meant to be. After an embarrassing photo, and the fact that I had written his name all over my brown desert boots, my little secret was eventually revealed.

The photo was actually a picture of him and his cousin, but I dreamt that one day it would be me standing beside him. In one crazy moment I wrote on the back of the photo, 'I wish it was me.' A year later, I had forgotten about it, only to be reminded when the photo found its way back, would you believe, into the hands of his cousin. What are the chances? Well, when it came to me and my dreamy so-called love life, the chances were huge. The maths textbook which once belonged to me and had the picture in it soon became his cousin's textbook. Let's just say that when he found out, it wasn't the fairy tale ending I was hoping for. It was my worst nightmare. I was sitting on the oval with my friends when he came up and yelled at me.

'I wish it was me!' He had found out about the photo, which meant he found out I liked him, which meant everyone would find out.

I felt like the world had suddenly tripled in size and I was the size of an ant, hoping someone would step on me and put me out of my misery. Unfortunately, that didn't happen. As you can imagine, the next few months were not exactly the best. I would have much preferred the ground to have swallowed me up. Instead I had to tolerate the taunts and teasing that came with such a revelation. Not surprisingly, he chose someone else.

Once again, things started to change. High school was over, and I needed to do something more than to stay and procreate. I didn't know exactly what that was, but I knew it wasn't staying in the Riverland. Things were changing and I didn't like what I saw. The most surprising was the change in attitude of the people I had once considered my friends, all because of my sister's relentlessness determination to give me a normal teenage life.

By my mid-teens I was old enough to travel to Adelaide on my own on the bus. It was something I would organise every year for a few weeks in the summer months. I would call my aunty, get her approval and book my bus ticket. By the time I turned eighteen, the options were even greater. Rather than going to the same nightclub every Saturday night, my sister, her friends and I used to travel to either Mildura, in

Victoria, or to Adelaide. During the week, I went to training or to the local pub in the evening.

I couldn't wait to turn eighteen. It meant I didn't need to use my fake ID to go out any more, but it also meant that I was allowed to drink, a teenager's dream. However, the night of my birthday wasn't the exact night I was hoping for. My friends were definitely going to do something to me, but I wasn't exactly sure what. They were not to be trusted when it came to someone celebrating a milestone. That was especially the case for me, because I was the youngest of the group. It started as an innocent coffee and something to eat at the local café. The café was not too far from my parents' house so you could walk there, which, by the way, I ended up doing by the end of the night. Let's just say I was lucky to have been wearing my bikini. It was a waiting game. I was waiting for something to happen and they were waiting for me to run, which I tried to do but was caught in the process. I was grabbed, stripped – thankfully not down to my birthday suit – and tied up, right in front of the café. After tying me up, my friend went to her car and grabbed a bucket of what could only be described as actual crap. She owned a takeaway shop and kept all the food waste from that day, which included egg, egg curry, rotten lettuce; you name it, I wore it. She grabbed the bucket and launched all of its contents over me and there was a lot of it. It stank, which basically meant I stank. But that was not the embarrassing bit. She asked Patrick – yes, the same Patrick I've mentioned before – if he would mind hosing me off before they untied me. He grabbed the hose and started spraying. While it might have been one of my fantasies that included Patrick, it wasn't quite in such a context. Embarrassed was an understatement. I could not believe they could do this and involve him. I was so pissed off. Even my dad knew what they were going to do, but kept it a secret, only suggesting that I think carefully about whether I wanted to go out with them or not. What kind of clue is that? I ended up walking home, because the smell was so bad that my sister wouldn't let me in the car. Never mind the curry that was stuck in my hair for two weeks, as long as the car didn't smell.

It was only during the day that living in the Riverland was so difficult. I had finished school, but had no job. I did, however, have a driver's licence and borrowing Dad's car whenever I wanted it meant I could also look for work. I really enjoyed art and graphics and I managed to get some work experience in Berri. It wasn't for long, but it gave me something to do. Not one to sit still, I always looked for opportunities to keep me busy. I managed to organise work experience at the Hindley Street police station. I was there for a week and got to experience many facets of the job. I remember the officers got me to watch over a teenager who had been caught stealing. I never knew it at the time, but that was to be the beginning of my counselling career. It was recommended that police work was something I should consider. It was definitely a consideration, but getting out of the Riverland was more important. I didn't think I had it in me to live there for another year.

8

A little town called Barmera – into the abyss

The best way to get a feel for a town is to walk there. Being only five minutes from my parents' home, the walk was not a difficult one. The striking thing was how quiet it was. It was one straight road that began at the golf course and ended at a T-junction leading to the main street. As I walked, out of the corner of my eye I could see the old Greek men occupying the park benches on the median strip. I didn't really want to talk to them, let alone acknowledge them. I tried to avoid eye contact but I could sense them staring and, feeling all eyes on me, I let out a '*Kalimera ti kanete* (Good morning, how are you?)' It made them happy, which was clearly the reason for my existence. But doing it meant I didn't have to hear about it when I got home, after they complained to my father for my rudeness. This is a perfect example of the unwritten rule that I talked about earlier. It's about perception, being seen to do the right thing, despite anything else.

Even the weather in the Riverland was relentless. When it was hot, it was ridiculously hot; you couldn't even step out your front door, for fear it would kill you. My family and I used to spend all day inside with the air conditioner on, until at least three or four o'clock, when we would finally make our way to the outside world. That was a common occurrence, as we were without air conditioning for a very long time before that. We would take the TV outside, using the extension cord so the TV could reach the plug inside. We would have our own outdoor cinema, taking the cushions, blankets and snacks outside, like our own private Idaho. Yes, it was hot, but it was also fun, and we made the best out of a bad situation. We didn't stay out all night, only until the temperature dropped and before we became dinner for the mosquitoes. Once inside, we would sleep on the cold floor and keep all the doors open. We never worried about people breaking in. It was just too hot and back then it never happened, not like it does now, and it was heat that people were mainly concerned with. However, on the other side of that were the cold winters. The mornings were the worst. The cold would just go straight through you, no matter how many layers you had on. It would pierce your body like a knife. The cold brought on a tingling sensation that reached every fibre of your being. There was no escaping it, especially because we only had a little gas heater at the time. I can't remember exactly when we got the air conditioner but it definitely would've been when I was a teenager.

During the summer months, going outside in the middle of the day could've been seen as a suicide mission, not for the untrained. Later in the afternoon was better and much safer. Any earlier and you might have not come back alive. But my sister and I, and sometimes our brother, didn't care. I much preferred to risk the scorching heat than to sitting inside watching endless hours of cricket. I didn't care if Warnie bowled 4/49 or if Waugh hit a six; that was not going to cool me down.

We only had one TV, so it was first in, first served. That was the one my brother always seemed to win. In that instance, drawing, writing and playing cards were the choices of entertainment, not forgetting the old favourite, the jigsaw puzzle.

I remember swimming with my siblings at the lake. As there were no beaches where we lived, the lake was our beach. On one particularly hot day, my siblings convinced me that the best time to swim was through the thunderstorms. I remember them dragging me – okay, maybe not dragging, but taking me there. As we immersed ourselves in the water, the clouds started to darken. That meant thunderstorms and lighting were just around the corner. It was the middle of the day, but the clouds made it seem like it was night. Not long after, the drops started to fall, and I'm talking big drops. They got heavier, and then began the downpour. It was amazing to watch. It felt like you were getting your own private sky show. The water was so much cleaner back then. I cried the first time I experienced it, because I thought I was going to be struck by lighting and die, but clearly that never happened.

After I had done it a few times, it was the best, and I wanted to do it all the time. My parents were opposed to it, but that didn't matter; if my brother and sister were going to do it, so would I.

9

My first nightclub – thirteen, police, toilets, best hiding spot – what more could a girl ask for?

It was very important to my sister that I experience night life at a normal early age, without the curfew and without the guilt about staying out late. She didn't want me to encounter the same dramas she'd had with our dad. When I was about thirteen years old, my sister decided she was going to take me out. The nightclub was located in Berri, fifteen minutes away. It wasn't like the city clubs, it was smaller, not as glamorous, and you couldn't take two steps without seeing someone you knew, but it was the only place in town so, other than staying home, it was the place that everyone went to.

Like all nightclubs, the age of entry was eighteen, but rules were meant to be broken, right? So began my introduction to the world of nightclubs at the tender age of thirteen. Anyway, unlike these days, back in the day, nightclubs got busier a lot earlier – nine o'clock instead of midnight. To avoid the police asking for ID, the toilets were the best hiding spot; they would never check there. My sister and I would get there around quarter to nine, just before the police arrived, with enough time to smuggle me into the toilet cubicle until the coast was clear. I remember being in there for a good fifteen minutes, sometimes wondering whether my sister would come back at all, because it wouldn't have been the first time she had forgotten me.

It was quite the adrenalin rush at the time and quite the

conversation opener with my friends too. They weren't allowed to go out, and especially to the nightclub, until they were older and even then not all the time. This in itself proved how naïve the parents were, as if you needed to go to a nightclub to misbehave. For example, some would meet at Apex Park, which was a secluded area located on the other side of the lake. Others would lie that they were visiting friends, but instead they would be catching up with their boyfriend. It was another fine example of ignorance or living in oblivion. Sometimes I wasn't sure what some of those parents were thinking.

So, anyway, after spending fifteen minutes in the toilets, I was ready to party. Always the cautious, I never had an alcoholic drink. It was more about the rush of doing something so-called illegal. I was amongst all those adults, no longer thirteen but eighteen. It's funny how we want to grow up so quickly, do what the adults do, but as soon as we hit that age we want to go backwards.

During the day, the club resembled any other hotel bar, but at night it transformed into a whole other world. Each area was sectioned off, not literally but metaphorically. It appeared as if each nationality had its own corner, just like a boxing ring. The setting of the nightclub would be hard to believe if I didn't see it with my own eyes. The Aussies would be segregated on one side, the Greeks on the other. In fact, the Greek section was named the Athenian Corner, and while it was actually a mixture of Europeans, it was still predominantly governed by the Greeks. Even when I hit eighteen and started going out properly, the segregation rules remained.

Eventually, going to that place became something I felt I had to do rather than something I wanted to do. It was no longer fun, the novelty was over, or maybe I was over it; maybe it wasn't the place at all, maybe it was me. I had outgrown it and needed something more, which has become somewhat of a pattern through my adult years. But there was nothing else to do. You couldn't just go out for a coffee; there were no coffee shops. And you couldn't go shopping; the shops shut at 1 p.m.

Just surviving a normal day was almost impossible. The only saving grace I had was on Sundays, specifically in the winter months, when I would go to the soccer. Being old enough to drive, I didn't have to depend on Dad, but could go with my friends.

But that was only one day of the week for about nine months. The drive-in was also a highlight through the week, usually on a Friday or Sunday night, and yes, while it might have appeared there was no reason for me to complain about my life, there actually was.

For a town that had two supermarkets, a police station, post office, newsagency, library, two petrol stations and a bank, and appeared to operate in slow motion, people's mouths were on full speed. The gossip was relentless and while I could easily have been caught up in it, I didn't really want to. The town functioned on gossip: who did this, who said that, who slept with whom. There were always stories about someone. The worst part was it wasn't said behind closed doors, which is why it's called gossip, I guess. It was like being in an episode of *Desperate Housewives*. The main street was notorious for the ritual: the discussion of parties, weddings, and clubbing. The worst were the comments made about what people wore. Who cares? But they did, especially when going to church for Easter.

Easter was a big deal, and you couldn't get away with wearing the same outfit twice. That was especially the case when going to church over the two or three nights, which we often did. It meant you had to buy a new outfit or not go to church, and the latter was not an option. Going to church was like attending a fashion parade. Most people weren't there to worship or pray, but to show off how much money they had. I'm under no illusion that the same thing happens in the city, but I think it's much worse when everyone knows everyone and escape is not an option. There's a very funny post that gets shared on Facebook especially around Easter that states, 'Greek Fashion Week at a church near you.'

10

Growing up in Barmera – my sister, my hero!

Being the youngest of three children, I was always someone's little sister, never really having my own identity, which was all I really ever wanted. Unfortunately, that came much later in life. In the meantime, I lived vicariously through my sister. I wanted to be just like her. She was popular and everyone loved her, the life of the party, something I was not. I had friends I went out with but, as I eventually discovered, it was just about that – going out. And they weren't really my friends.

I couldn't wait for my sister to wake up on Sunday mornings, so I could hear her stories from the night before, because there was always a story. I was so envious, but I was only a teenager at the time.

As I said, everyone loved her. On a Saturday night, the phone would start ringing at 7 p.m. and didn't stop until she left the house. I thought my sister's popularity was brilliant. She was my hero, and while I was envious, I was never jealous. We were very different, after all. She was a lot more open than me. I was reserved, always the observer, which had more to do with trust than anything else. According to my sister, she paved the way. If it wasn't for her, I wouldn't have been allowed to go out. Having no curfew was all her doing.

I'm sure the oldest sibling of any family would agree with her, but being the youngest wasn't exactly a picnic either. It also has its disadvantages. 'Such as?' you might ask. Well, the pressure can often be on the youngest to succeed should the oldest not measure up to expectations, which in my family were very high.

The age gap was a disadvantage but once I got a bit older, my sister let me hang out with her friends, so it wasn't all bad. Of course, I would never have gone to a night club at thirteen if it hadn't been for my sister, so I guess she was right in some of the statements she made.

But the one thing I had that neither of my siblings had was my extraordinary ability to read people. I could tell within five minutes whether they were keepers or not. I'm sure it was genetics and not anything miraculous, but it always felt good when one of them would ask my opinion. I went with intuition back then. These days, I'm a little more reluctant and try not to do it at all, especially if asked. Nevertheless, it was something that kept the three of us connected, just like game days when we would spend endless hours in our pyjamas playing Scrabble or gin rummy. They were good times.

My father was really strict with my sister but she fought back, never giving up on what she wanted, and finally her relentlessness paid off. Having endured that constant battle, she didn't want me going through the same thing, so with every social opportunity that came her way, she made sure I was included.

On many occasions, there would be a tap on my window at midnight, with my sister calling, 'Vic, Vic, are you ready?' Ready was an understatement! I would bounce out of bed, at the same time trying to be as quiet as possible. But sometimes Dad would hear me, and out would come his little torch to check the time, and then came the questions: '*Pou pas tetia ora*? (Where are you going at this time of the night?)' Obviously I didn't have time to spell it out, but he knew, which meant my sister was going to get into trouble. I did feel bad, but I knew she was prepared to deal with it; she was tough.

According to my sister, I was ahead of my time, knowing what I wanted and going for it. Hating to admit it, I do have her to thank for that, as much as working it out for myself.

Living in a small Greek community, it was a given that you should marry one of your own, but that wasn't for me, God no! I was ambitious. I wanted to have a successful career. I wanted my success to define me, and while I have been successful in all my chosen careers, I have since learnt that success should never define you. Whether you are making a living, playing sport competitively, or volunteering, it should never define who you are. All these things are things we do; they're not who we are. I believe we do have a purpose in life – we have been sent here to do something – but it's not who we are.

Unfortunately, this ambition, or obsession, depending on how you look at it, consumed me for a long time. It has probably only been in the last few years that I have chosen to do what makes me happy as opposed to what makes me successful.

11

Teenage years, high school – being a teenager can be hard

My childhood was like most, the only real difference being that my family lived in a Housing Trust home, which my parents now own. While that may not be all that uncommon, it was in the eyes of the Greek community. Not that it mattered where we lived, because my parents made it a home.

My siblings insisted that I was spoilt because I was the youngest, but it wasn't my fault – I was born last. I was spoilt, but there were also high expectations of me.

Speaking to some of my other Greek friends, it seems my father wasn't the only one who put high expectations on his children. It's almost like, in addition to a blanket, food and the minor necessities when travelling to Australia by boat, there was also a book called *How To Raise Greek Children*. Every time we did something my dad didn't approve of, which was most of the time, he used to say, '*Tha me pethanete* (You're going to kill me).'

I am, however, pleased to report that there has been no death. He's eighty-two years old and still going strong. If you really want to know what it's like growing up in a Greek household, just watch *My Big Fat Greek Wedding*. Ninety-five per cent of it is accurate. These days we love making fun of what my dad used to say, even guessing his response when we tell him something.

There was a lot of pressure on me as a kid and now, as an adult, I would tell my child-self to find someone to talk to rather than holding it all inside. That is why I like training kids. I want to teach them that you don't have to be the best; you just have to do your best. And to also tell them not to let anyone tell them they can't do something.

I think it was all those little moments that motivated me to succeed. I was determined from a very young age and that has translated through to adulthood. If someone told me I couldn't, I made sure I could. The irony is that I lost this attitude when I needed it most, as I entered my teens and early twenties. Luckily I found myself getting it back once I got into the martial arts, but first I had to endure high school and the various individuals who made it difficult for me.

I started high school in 1986 and on the first day I got my head flushed. It was a tradition that I didn't think actually happened to girls, but I guess I was wrong. I'm not sure of the exact details, morning or afternoon, but I remember being chased, pulled into the boys' toilets, head under the cistern and flush!

Could the day have gotten any worse? Yes! At the end of the day, I forgot where my bus stop was. Luckily my brother found me. Not the most memorable day, but definitely the most unforgettable. Unfortunately, the bullying did not stop there, but what doesn't kill you… You know the rest!

My high schooling was interrupted when my father took the whole family to Greece to visit our relatives. I didn't want to go, probably because I resented the fact that my relatives got to share in what my parents had worked so hard for. I believed they simply didn't deserve it. In order to escape this insanity (the weird relatives we were staying with, the way we were playing happy families), we siblings spent time going to the beach and visiting other relatives. We basically spent time with people who wanted to spend time with us. It was there that I learnt how to play backgammon. Don't ask me to play now, though; I'd have absolutely no idea.

So as you can imagine, returning to school was easier said than done. After three months away, you don't know what to expect. Friendships may change, situations may change, and they did. I wasn't really sure how it all happened, how it actually began, it just did, and they were relentless. There was a group of girls who decided I was going to be their target. Every day for the rest of that year they called me Smelly. Ironically it had nothing to do with how I smelled. It was just their way of tormenting me, and it worked. They were as regular as clockwork and the more I tried to get away, the more often they would appear. I complained to the teachers but to no avail.

On one occasion, they even set me up. After hiding my bag and then their own, they went to the teacher claiming I had taken their bags and hidden them. Who do you think she believed? Let's just say it wasn't me. I was actually reprimanded for it. And then we wonder why kids take matters into their own hands. Even my so-called friends didn't try to help, and I say 'so-called' because it's in such moments that you find out who your friends really are. In hindsight, I realise I should have got the message back then. It took up to adulthood for me to discover that if your friends make you look like an idiot on more than one occasion, you are an idiot!

Perhaps they had their reasons but as a child that is not something I thought of. I was also too scared to confront them (this coming from a martial arts black belt – the irony) and telling my parents was out of the question.

Don't feel sorry for me, though, because I too was a bully. I was in my last year of primary school and gave one of my classmates a very hard time. She didn't actually do anything wrong, not that it matters if she did. It was more about me trying to fit in and be like everyone else. Thinking about it now, I can't believe I could be so nasty, but as you know, fate caught up with me a year later and the bully became the bullied.

12

Leaving Barmera – my prayers had been answered

Let's get this party started! You couldn't wipe the smile off my face. I was leaving the Riverland once and for all, never to return. Bon voyage! It was possibly the best day of my life. I received two letters of acceptance: one from the North Adelaide School of Arts and the other from the School of Graphic Arts.

When I received the news I was moving, I felt twenty feet tall. I was on top of the world and nothing was going to bring me down; not those insignificant people who had ridiculed me, no one. How young and foolish I was. I was running and I didn't even know it.

While I was excited about moving, I was also somewhat reluctant. The move meant living with my brother, Sam. The last time we lived together we didn't get along. Actually that's an understatement – we used to fight all the time – but it was going to be different now. There was a time when I might not have felt so confident.

When I was five years old, I had to wear a patch over my eye after my brother almost blinded me. It wasn't his fault entirely. As a child, I was quite the pain. I was always in my siblings' way and was just the annoying little sister. On this particular occasion, I was doing something to annoy my brother – I can't remember exactly what – while he was trying to hit a golf ball. He wasn't a golfer; it was just something to do. Well, he asked me to get out the way, not once, twice, but three times, and of course I didn't listen. So he whacked the ball, and it hit me right in the eye. He didn't mean to do it, and he did feel really bad about it. Let's just say there was a very quick trip to Emergency, and Sam was left feeling pretty sorry for himself. The biggest needle I had ever seen was injected under my eye, and I had to wear a bandage plus a patch. It made me look like an extra on the movie *Pirates of the Caribbean*, but apart from that, there was no damage to my sight, thank God.

Childhood stories aside, we were both older now and trying to have a better relationship. I think his departure to Adelaide a few years earlier made all the difference. Of course, he had to act like the big brother and set ground rules, but once again, rules were meant to be broken. Making the adjustment was difficult, especially because I went from living in a house to living in a small unit. However, that was not the biggest challenge; finding my way around Adelaide was. I had a car – I took my sister's car when she went to Greece – but apart from college, the only place I knew how to get to was my cousin's house, and that was during the day, because the roads looked so different at night.

Buses were another great way to learn your way around Adelaide; they would take a lot of the roads I wouldn't normally take. The only time driving might have been a problem was when I had to do work experience. That was when my brother was very helpful. Once I had the details for the location, we would both take a drive on the weekend to make sure I knew how to get there, ready for Monday.

Being child number three in my family also meant that I didn't need to learn the skill of cooking, unlike my sister who had to iron, cook, make beds, and anything else that was required. But why did I need to learn? For moments like these. Having already lived on his own for some time, my brother had to learn how to cook. The only problem was that he only knew how to cook one dish: spaghetti and beef. Apart from takeaway, it was the only dish we used to eat, 350 days a year, until my sister moved in. I swore I would never eat it again.

Thursdays were normally shopping day, but my brother didn't get a chance to go during the day so he had to go at night. However, one night he decided we would have something different, chicken. So he said to me, 'I'm quickly going to do the shopping. All you have to do is look after the chicken' – a fairly easy request to follow, if you know how to cook, which clearly I did not. Suffice to say, not only did I burn the chicken, we also had to throw out the pot. My brother never asked me to look after the dinner again. I can't imagine why. On a more positive note, it could have been worse: I could have burnt the place down. But my brother actually blamed himself for leaving. He loves telling that story.

I enjoyed the college experience, the buzzing of students, the freedom to come and go as you pleased and the good friends that I made along the way. My brother never had any problem with me going out, as long as I studied hard and made good grades. He never pressured me to perform well. I put that pressure on myself. I accepted nothing less than a credit. I never wanted to feel inadequate or stupid like I had done in the past and, to my surprise, I was getting the grades. So my reward was to go out on the weekend.

Apart from my friends from college and some existing friends older than me, the only other friends I had were my cousin Vicky's friends. My cousin had the same name as me. We Greeks are named after our grandparents. The first female is named after the grandmother on the father's side; the second female in the same family gets her name from the mother's side.

Vicky was a hard act to follow. She had the life I wanted. She was working, had a boyfriend, and had so many friends; they just loved her and still do. She was mean to me, though; she'd tell me what to do, especially when driving. 'You're not changing gears properly,' and 'You're going too slow.' I never answered back, because I felt intimidated. My cousin was my idol, so I didn't want to rock the boat.

I found that part of my life the hardest. What I also learnt is that you should always try and make your own friends. I didn't know how I was supposed to act, feel or exist, so I tried to change my attitude and personality to fit in. It didn't make it better; it actually made it much worse. Not only were my cousin's friends unhappy with my attitude, so was my cousin. Perhaps that was just the first sign of my unhappiness to come. I changed back, back to the way I was in the Riverland, but I got much of the same response. I felt I was stuck. No matter what I did, I felt I couldn't win, so I plodded along and just tried to do the best I could. On the other hand, the fact that I didn't have a curfew made me lucky compared to some of the others. I was also the perfect excuse to stay out late, which was used quite a lot, but I didn't mind, because I got to learn more about my cousin's friends. An education I will never forget.

When we used to go out, my cousin always hooked up with good-looking guys, but I also had my fair share, not as consistent, but regular enough. Back then, hooking up meant that you had a good night. But hooking up didn't mean sex; it just meant kissing. We were good Greek girls and sex wasn't in our vocabulary. And anyway, we were too scared of our parents finding out. Mind you, I did have an advantage. My parents were 222 kilometres away, so how would they find out? But I didn't; I felt I was still too young for such an important decision. And we still had fun.

Vicky and I were close as kids, but our relationship went up and down over time. At one stage we didn't speak to each other for about three years. I felt I was never able to express myself, always hiding behind a tough exterior. I was raised to believe that showing emotion meant weakness, which is what brought on our feud.

It all began when my cousin announced she was seeing the man who is now her husband and they were planning to get married. It shocked and stunned me, not because I didn't want her to be happy, but because I believed that she was marrying for the wrong reason. I was worried that my cousin was settling, that the only reason she was getting married was because she thought she would never get the opportunity again. I was wrong. Her husband turned out to be a really great guy and they're so good together. However, instead of explaining how I really felt, I decided it was my cousin's partner who was going to be my target – not the smartest move. I made life for my cousin and her partner very difficult, because what affected him, obviously also affected her.

The result was the opposite of what I wanted. The claws came out, especially from my side. I couldn't understand why my cousin couldn't see it from my point of view. After many heated arguments, which were simple raw emotion from two people who cared about each other, there was no going back. It went on for three years and it was my biggest regret. Not only did I lose three years of friendship but, more importantly, I wasn't there for her when her mother passed away. Thankfully, our time apart enabled me to find the words I so desperately wanted to say to Vicky back then, but couldn't. The relationship took time to rebuild and it's become what it once was again, perhaps even better.

The place I shared with my brother Sam was a rented unit on Regency Road in Prospect. We spent a year living there, but then got to the point where it was time to move. We needed to find a house, and because we didn't have the money to buy one, we rented from our uncle. The house was on a corner block, on the western side of Adelaide, in a suburb called Royal Park. It was not the most attractive, nor the easiest to clean, but what it lacked in attractiveness, it gained by getting the title Party Central.

I was hardly the domesticated kind back then – even now I struggle – and really neither was my brother. So every Friday without fail someone would drop in and suddenly it became a party. There were many empty Scotch bottles. In fact, when I first moved in with my brother, he had quite the collection, like trophies standing proudly on the mantelpiece. Living there was great, but paying the bills not so much, especially from my small wage of $5.45 per hour at the time. But the small wage never deterred me from a night out. It didn't matter if you were sick or broke, not going out was never an option.

13

Playing soccer

On Tuesday nights, my cousin Vicky used to play indoor soccer. She told me they needed a goalkeeper, so the team trained me to be one. It wasn't an easy position to play, but I got used to it and really started to enjoy it. I endured many injuries, the most memorable being two sprained thumbs, but I didn't care. I loved the game.

During one of our games, I learnt that a new girls' outdoor team was looking for players. I put my hand up straight away. 'Finally something of my own,' I thought. The team was called Norwood All Blacks. I loved it but obstacles got in the way of my continuing with it.

Training was in the north-eastern area, and living in the western suburbs meant a forty-five-minute commute to the training sessions. I played for the Norwood All Blacks for one year but then had to stop; the distance was just too far. It was also because I didn't know the area very well and was worried that if something happened, such as if the car broke down, I wouldn't be able to find my way back. It had already happened once, when I first drove up there and ended up getting lost. I knocked on someone's door to get directions and instead what I got was a crazy guy who started yelling at me. 'What do you want? What do you want?' He started following me back to the car, but I kept my composure – that is, until I got into the car, locked the doors, thanked God I wasn't going to be a dead body in an episode of *Criminal Minds* and sped off like a bat out of hell.

Neither that incident nor the distance deterred me from playing soccer. I just played for a different outdoor team and still continued to play indoor soccer. I felt like I had finally found my feet. Unfortunately, instead of being happy for me, my siblings were the complete opposite. They thought I was playing too much, and socialising too much, and that basically I needed to spend more time at home. Well, they got their wish: I stopped playing soccer. Granted it didn't happen straight away, but it did happen. Perhaps they wished it so much that it came true, or was it my attitude that was changing? My attitude was becoming very negative. I was becoming depressed.

However, I wasn't ready to give up the game. How can you give up something you love? And I did love it. I was also good at it. In fact, I was actually promoted to a first division team until, of course, my big unfiltered mouth got me demoted and eventually kicked out. I was provoked, but maybe I overreacted.

It was just another practice night for Sunday's game and, just like any other night, parents were sitting behind the goalposts. The parents would normally sit and watch, keeping their opinions to themselves. However, on this particular occasion, sitting behind my goalposts was a very vocal parent directing his rants at me about my 'lack of technique'. Granted it wasn't one of my greatest practice sessions, but that's why it's called practice. Anyway this parent kept going on and on, and it didn't look like he was planning to stop anytime soon. I could only be patient for so long and then it happened. Before my brain reached my mouth, I said, 'Do you think you want to shut the fuck up?' Like it was a question!

We really do need a rewind button in life. Instead it felt like the tape was stuck and I kept hearing it over and over again. Clearly, in hindsight I know I was wrong to react that way, but seriously, how much can one person take? I was angry! More so because the 'gentleman' who complained to the coach was also on the committee, so that was that. Despite turning up to training, I was no longer asked to play. The players would receive a phone call if they weren't required for the game, which in my case became most weekends. So the promotion became a demotion in the blink of an eye.

I suddenly learned that sports such as soccer were not governed by skill, but more by politics. At least I got to enjoy my fifteen minutes of fame. Being in a first division team was what players strived for, so no matter how short-lived, I always had that. Ironically, after being dropped, I actually enjoyed playing for the third division team more, as I was able to showcase my skill a lot more.

That was the last year I would play outdoor soccer. My passion for soccer had begun to fade when the distance forced me to change teams; I just didn't know it at the time. However, the political crossfire that was the straw that broke the camel's back proved to be a major turning point in my life. I was about to find a new and ultimately much more satisfying passion.

14

Why martial arts? – About a boy!

Long before I started playing soccer, even before I left the Riverland, I had begun training in martial arts.

It wasn't common for a female to take up martial arts and I have often been asked why I started in the first place. 'Did something happen to you in your childhood?' The reason is simple. It was all about a boy! Patrick – the same boy I had fallen in love with all those years ago in school. My brother told me that Patrick did martial arts with him, so what was a girl to do? Join up, of course!

It was hopeless, or more like I was hopeless. I couldn't get any of the combinations. The moves required certain finesse and I had none. It also required the use of both sides of the brain, but there was no left brain/right brain for me; there was really no brain at all. But what did that matter? I wasn't there for the art; I was there for the boy.

Having absolutely no idea what I was doing was not as embarrassing as having Patrick knowing I was really there for him. He wore that ridiculous, cute, frustrating smirk on his face, which basically said, 'I know you're only coming here for me, and I think it's cute.' I didn't care. Maybe then he would know how far I would go for him, and he would want me as much as I wanted him. But how could he know? He wasn't a mind reader. Was I being that obvious? Probably. But once again it was my mind playing tricks on me and Patrick basically messing with my already messed-up head. Patrick would pick me up and throw me over his shoulder, like some caveman claiming his woman which, by the way, was absolutely fine with me. My speechlessness provided him with some light entertainment, as I couldn't put two syllables together. He used to make me so nervous. It was the anxiety all over again. Sometimes I would replay our conversations over and over in my head, making sure I hadn't said anything stupid and if I had, what should I have said? Oh, to be young again.

After a couple of years of training, I became quite good in the martial arts, even teaching some of the younger students. I taught them everything I knew, from correcting their technique to telling them to pull their heads in when they were playing up, and that happened a lot. Overall, though, they were a talented bunch of kids. The shocker for me was when they started to emulate my bad behaviour. I hate to admit it but there were times when I disrespected my instructor. That was not allowed, but I did it anyway. When the students started to do it, I quickly changed my behaviour and told them to do the same.

I continued with martial arts in the Riverland for a few more years, four to be exact, before I decided to give it up. Things had changed. The boy was gone; he had gained his black belt and left. And to be perfectly honest, I wasn't that into it any more, so there was no real reason to stay. I left with a brown belt black tip (one stripe away from a black belt), which was quite a satisfying achievement. Once again I needed more and had my sights on moving to the city. I quit training, quit my part-time job in the supermarket, applied to a couple of colleges and the rest is history. However, before I moved, there were a couple of other love interests.

15

Love interests

I met my first boyfriend at the local disco. Then, after only a short time, I met a friend of his who wanted to be more than a friend. Unfortunately for me, they both had the same name – what are the odds? In any case, Con and Con were friends. They both lived in the same town and went to the same school. I was young and naïve and quite scared of the whole relationship thing. The examples I had seen of relationships thus far had not proven successful. I had not grown up with a great male role model, which is probably one of the reasons I always had my guard up. That didn't stop either of them.

I didn't make it easy for the first Con. He was the gentleman and I was the loud obnoxious one, the one who would want to get into fights and who especially didn't like the man, or in this case the boy, standing up for her. Ultimately, I think that's the reason we broke up; that plus the fact that I was the wrong kind of Greek (not Cypriot Greek, just Greek). I haven't seen him in over a decade, so I hope he's happy.

Now the other Con definitely had me fooled, or was I just naïve? How was I supposed to know he was interested? He never gave me any hints or maybe he did but I didn't see them. We used to have so much fun together. I recently found out that most people thought we would end up together. How was it that everyone else knew but me? Was I that blind or was it just ignorance?

We first met on the bus travelling from Adelaide to the Riverland and it wasn't too long before it felt like we had known each other for years. In fact, I think it was on that occasion that we almost got kicked off the bus for being too loud. At the time he was studying in Adelaide to be a PE teacher and I was still living in the Riverland, so our forms of communication were writing letters and using the family phone. We would talk for ages, one or two hours, and write two, four, six page letters about what was going on in our lives. He always used to make me laugh. We would go out and get up to the most mischievous things.

But that all changed as soon as he told me he was interested. Presenting me with a rose he said, 'By the end of this night I'm going to kiss you.' I nearly shit myself.

I wasn't sure how to react, so of course I took the hard cold approach, not even contemplating the possibility. I told him that I thought it would affect our friendship, and ultimately it did. I never heard from him or saw him again. At the time, I couldn't understand why it was such a problem. Always seeing things in black and white, it hit me years later that I had hurt him. He showed me his vulnerable side, heart on sleeve, cards on the table and instead of listening and taking it in, my defences went up and I dismissed his declaration like it was nothing. What a fool. However, on the other side of that is my feeling that he could've fought for it, fought for me, but I guess we were both young and both scared.

That same night, I told my friends about what had happened and how Con had handed me a rose. They weren't very sympathetic. In fact, even though what they did next was funny, it was actually at my expense, and of course Con's, but I laughed it away. Getting into my car at the end of the night, I noticed a few roses attached to my wipers, mirror, and bonnet of my car. I didn't think anything of it and just drove home. It was late, I was tired and probably slightly intoxicated and just wanted to go to sleep. The next morning my mum said to me, 'Where did all these roses come from?'

I walked outside to see the car had not just roses it on it, but rose bushes. I found out later that after I'd told them the story, they'd travelled to Renmark, attacked a few rose bushes and put them on my car.

After Patrick, Con and Con, I met Mark. I couldn't actually imagine meeting anyone else after that. Everything seems so dramatic when you're twenty-one, but that's how I felt. Thankfully the universe had other ideas. I met Mark when his friend started seeing my cousin, Vicky. We were chaperones for them and often found ourselves listening to music while the other two were getting busy with their own activities. So what started out as two people doing a favour for their friends, or relative in my case, was the beginning of an unlikely friendship. I never looked at him as anything more than just a friend but then something changed, and it was the same for him. Given this was now Vicky's new group of friends, we always saw each other when we were out, and that smile just did something to me. He looked at me like I was the only one in the room. Like Con used to do. I remember one night we were out in a nightclub just sitting around and talking. One minute there was a whole group of us, then there was just the two to us, and to my surprise he gently leaned over and gave me a kiss on the cheek. 'What was that for?' I asked, and his response was, ''Cause I felt like it.'

I wanted him so much at the time. We had this connection that I hadn't felt in so long, but there was someone else in the picture, someone I thought I couldn't compete with. Whatever our relationship was, it was intense; something you couldn't put into words. There was definitely a connection, and Mark felt it too.

An opportunity did present itself, but it wasn't the right time. I was standing at the foot of the dance floor in one of Adelaide's most prominent nightclubs in the late 90s, just talking to a friend. As I scanned the room, I suddenly saw him from afar, but decided not to approach. I didn't want to look desperate, and anyway I thought he should approach me. A few minutes later, I felt his head on my shoulder. My whole body came alive; it was like electricity, and in that moment I considered given myself to him.

But I also had to be honest with myself. I would always be his second choice and I was better than that. I would always want more than he could give, and I wasn't willing to settle. The thought of fighting for him did cross my mind, but I never did. I wanted the fairy tale and still do. But it took the building of an emotional wall, being alone, set-ups, blind dates, speed dating and a lot of soul searching to get me past this point.

I was very unhappy in my twenties and that was reflected in my attitude. I was always angry, but the crazy thing was, I never even knew why. The anger didn't appear straight away; it manifested over time, after Patrick, after Mark, after numerous dates, after a few years in Adelaide. It started while I was an apprentice.

16

My first job – what doesn't kill you makes you stronger

I was so excited when I got my first job. I was still in trade school, with a couple of months to go, but the offer seemed too good to be true – and it was! When I received the call, my brother was right there with me to enjoy the moment, but the moment was to be short-lived. The job was for a graphic reproducer, working in a darkroom and taking loads of pictures. I was not and never had been afraid of interviews. I thought I had a pretty good vibe about the place and the people who worked there. I wasn't entirely wrong; most of the people were great. As for the others, not even a crystal ball could've predicted what I was in for. The job was far from what I expected. In fact, it was a complete nightmare. As an apprentice, I expected I was going to do all the crappy jobs, but my boss took that to a whole new level. It was up to the employers to teach the apprentice, but the only skills I picked up were exceptional cleaning skills. Great, if I was going to be a cleaner but not so great for a graphic reproducer.

The worst thing about the job – and there were many – was the daily threats I received from my boss. He was crazy! Or maybe he was really messed up and that's how he dealt with it, but either way there was no excuse for his behaviour. It began with threats of physical violence, such as threatening to smash my head against the wall, and verbal taunts, name-calling, 'stupid', 'dumb'. In fact, it got so bad that I wasn't allowed to sit down and eat lunch; I had to do it standing up. My boss would get so angry that I thought the veins in his neck would explode. He was very unpredictable and that was the scariest thing of all, because you didn't know what was coming next. I was always waiting for the one time that his verbal taunts would turn physical, but thankfully it didn't come. The taunts went on for about three years, so it was always a relief when he was away sick, or on annual leave. Those were good days. I dreaded getting up in the morning to go to work and back then apprentices weren't as protected as they are now. I couldn't really tell anyone either. If I'd mentioned it to my brother, he probably would have belted him, and I certainly didn't want to stress him out, so I kept it to myself.

In order to deal with this craziness, one of my colleagues would make jokes about what the boss might do next. He joked that he would come armed with a gun and start shooting everyone and because the darkroom was closest to the entry, I would be first. Of course, it was not funny, but we were just trying to make light of a crazy situation.

Despite this craziness, my Scottish colleague Dave was always there to turn a bad situation into something good. He would impersonate the boss, pretending to scream abuse at me. I would laugh till I cried, but that's what got me through the difficult days. I didn't really know how to stand up for myself. I was twenty years old and raised to work and not ask questions or answer back. My best ally was a guy named Brenton. After he left the job, things got worse.

By the third year, I had developed a greater resilience. The torments happened every day but, over time, I learned how to deal with them. The saying 'What doesn't kill you makes you stronger' rang true, and that was certainly the case here. Don't get me wrong. I wasn't strong every day. I just learned to cope better. Finally, I was able to stand up to him, because I was no longer afraid. I realised that there was nothing else he could do to me that he hadn't already done. Now I had the power and it was a good feeling.

I did speak to my teachers about it, but given I was so close to completing my apprenticeship, there was no point in making waves, but now I wish I had. What would you have done? Stay and just put up with it, or leave and risk not finding another apprenticeship? That's where I was. I think it was more than that, though. I think deep down I was worried that I would have to go back to the country, and that was simply not an option. I wish I had been strong enough to do something about it, but I just kept going, which I guess also showed strength.

The good news is I survived, but unfortunately my health was not so lucky. It began with a headache, then multiple headaches, then it travelled to my stomach. Clearly there was something wrong. I went to see the doctor and was told it was a stomach ulcer brought on by stress. I was shocked by the diagnosis but not surprised. How could anyone put up with what I'd had to put up with and not get sick? There wasn't a lot I could do about it. Back then, if I'd put stress as a reason for sick leave, it would've gone on my permanent records, and it would have been harder to get another job. So I plodded along, working as many hours as I could. The more hours I worked, the quicker I could finish my apprenticeship, and that's all I wanted, to get that piece of paper and get the hell out of there.

My wish was granted, but not exactly in the way I expected. The business was closed! Fortunately I got my apprenticeship documents at the same time. The day I was told about the closure was bitter-sweet. On one hand, I was glad to be getting out of there, but at the same time I didn't know what I was supposed to do next. I thought the few skills I had would be enough to get me another job, but I didn't know where or how.

17

My first overseas trip – on my own

Having barely survived the apprenticeship, I decided it was time to stand on my own two feet. I was living with my brother and sister and felt like I had no control over my own life. I needed to learn to assert myself. The only way I knew how to do that was to go away, as far away as possible.

With no job prospects, it was time to see the world and what better place to start but the United States of America. It was my first overseas trip on my own. I was twenty-five years old and while these days that sounds old for someone's first overseas trip, it's not when you come from a Greek family. The decisions were not made easily, nor were they taken on easily. But to my surprise, my parents accepted them – not that they had a choice – and that was that.

I had always dreamt about going to the States, attending a red carpet event like the Oscars or the Grammys…one day! Unfortunately, it wasn't this day, but I still haven't given up hope that it will happen. I believed that if I wanted to be someone or do something, America was the place to be.

The trip was indescribable. It was a three-week bus tour. Of course there were a few hiccups, which were to be expected, the first being personality clashes between me and my roommate. Imagine this opinionated, loud-mouthed wog, who had no filter when it came to expressing her opinion – just in case you're wondering, that was me – and an Englishwoman who had clearly only ever travelled on her own and lived on her own, which basically meant that things were on her terms…but not this time!

Heather and I were from different worlds, no similarities, from different hemispheres. Heather was upper middle-class English and I was western suburbs Greek; Heather was cup of English tea and I was black coffee; Heather got up early and I liked sleeping in. It seemed the relationship was doomed from the start, but stranger things have happened. Despite our differences, we eventually got along, knowing that no one was going to back down; we met in the middle and Heather ended up being one of the funniest women I had ever met. She liked shopping, as I did, and she also liked to express her opinion on everything – a match made in heaven.

On one particular occasion, we had been on and off the bus for about two weeks and there was a particularly odd smell coming from the back of the bus. At the time we couldn't pinpoint exactly where it was coming from, but there was definitely something there. The smell became too much and no one was saying anything, so I stepped up. I lost the plot, forcing the bus driver to stop the bus and find out where the smell was coming from. Once everyone was escorted off the bus, it wasn't long before we found the culprit, an overweight man who had not changed his underwear for the entire two weeks. The bus driver, bless him, bought him a new pair of underpants and shorts and asked him to get rid of or possibly burn the pair he'd been wearing. I would have been more sympathetic if he'd been living on the streets, but clearly that was not the case. If he could afford a holiday, he could certainly afford a pair of underpants. When the bus driver approached me, I actually thought I was in trouble, but it was actually the opposite – he thanked me for doing something about it.

The trip was a real eye-opener and one of the biggest things I learned was that I had the ability to travel on my own. I remember being at the airport saying goodbye to my family, getting on the plane and then thinking this was the first time I was going to be alone, on my own. What a rush of emotion! I was scared but also excited. I couldn't believe I was doing it. I was travelling to the other side of the world, and the only one who was looking after me was me. It was quite a significant time. I could feel myself growing stronger. I had never done anything like this before – there was always that back-up – but finally I got to see what I was made of.

I returned from the States in September. Was I happy about it? Not really, because I had experienced something amazing and knew that there was a whole other world out there. Unfortunately, a world that had to wait, because I had my brother's wedding to attend and be part of in November.

At the time, thanks to everything being so large in the States, I had gained nine kilos of additional weight that I did not need. However, at the time, I knew of no way of dropping it within two months. Now is a very different story. I did join a gym and participated in a few gym classes, but I needed more than that. Much to my dismay, the weight remained and I looked hideous in the bridesmaid's dress that was never going to happen again. My unhappiness also made its debut at the wedding. After getting very drunk and quite verbal towards certain relatives, I ended up being thrown out of the vehicle, shoes and all. Thankfully, we're all on talking terms again and no one ever brings up that incident. I put it down to being young, dumb and angry.

I never thought I had a problem; it was everyone around me who had the problem. At the time it seemed only my brother Sam was honest enough to tell me the truth, but he used to say it to me all the time, so I just stopped listening. My sister would make comments, but to no avail. It took me a long time to admit that I had a problem. Going out was a recipe for disaster, especially for the guys who used to approach me. I couldn't work out why they were being such wankers, but it wasn't them; it was me. When I was out with my sister, the guys who approached us couldn't believe we were related, let alone sisters.

After much continuous soul-searching, I couldn't deny there was a problem. I discovered that a bad attitude and being angry comes from unhappiness within. I clearly didn't like myself, let alone love myself, which is the key ingredient for someone loving you. I missed out on having relationships, both romantic and platonic, not that I thought about that at the time. But as the years passed me by, I slowly realised, and had to admit that I wanted what a lot of people had – someone to love and to love me back. Before that realisation, I had somehow convinced myself that if I showed my vulnerability, it would end badly and I would get hurt. In a nutshell, I was scared. Most importantly, I was afraid of losing my identity. What I didn't realise was that if you are with the right person, you won't lose anything; instead you'll gain by bringing the best out in each other. Perhaps talking to someone might have helped, but I wasn't a talker back then, and sometimes find it hard even now.

18

I break down – everyone ends up in a dark place one way or another: where am I, how did I get there and how did I get out?

It was about this time that I had my first meltdown, breakdown, whatever you want to call it. Everything that could go wrong did go wrong. I felt like a person possessed, like something had taken control of me, and the most frightening part was, I didn't know how long it would last.

My brother's kettle and the kitchen tiles were the first casualties of my breakdown. I remember standing at the stove making a coffee, waiting for the kettle to boil, but I'd forgotten a very important element of coffee making – the water! It was one of those old kettles with a lid, and all of a sudden I heard BOOM! The lid shot off and hit the ceiling. Thankfully, the kettle survived, apart from the burnt bit on the bottom.

The tiles were not as dramatic. I was just standing at the kitchen sink, doing something – not sure what – when suddenly, two or three tiles just came off the wall. It began to feel like anything I had contact with was falling to pieces. I felt like I was a character in the movie *The Exorcist*.

The most significant of all was my dad's car. He had one of those old-school Valiants, maroon colour. Anyway, while my parents were visiting from the country, I borrowed their car. It wasn't the first time I had driven it, so I was quite surprised at what happened next. Given it had no power steering and so drove like a truck, and given its size, some could be excused for not wanting to drive it, but it didn't faze me.

But on this particular day, I may have over-thought my confidence, because as I was turning into the car park of my cousin Vicky's salon, I heard a loud bang! I ended up hitting a pole and denting the side doors. Of course, I began freaking out. The feeling of nausea took over my body; I just wanted to throw up. What was I supposed to say? How was I going to explain it? I did something I had never done before, and clearly wasn't good at, and that was lie. Don't get me wrong; I have told white lies like when my cousin and I wanted to stay out longer and we said that the elevator was stuck, but that was nothing like this. I told my dad that it happened while I was at the shopping centre. I would have got away with it, had my brother not got involved. He knew the security guard, which meant there would be video footage, so the truth would have come out eventually. At that point, it was just too much for me to take. I just burst into tears and told my dad the truth. Surprisingly, he was very understanding. He basically said, 'Don't worry about it. It's only a car. It will be all right,' but it wasn't – not for a long time.

19

The printing place – the higher the rise, the harder the fall

Do you remember a time in your life when you convinced yourself that everything was going exactly how you planned, but the truth of the matter is that you were barely hanging on? Well, that was me.

So what do you do when you want to ignore the problem? Let your work consume you, of course. In December that year I got a new job. Keeping with the printing industry, I started working for one of the largest printing companies in Adelaide, working as a supervisor.

The first year I worked like a demon. I saved up $10,000, which I used to put a deposit on the unit where I now live. I was a hard worker and it was noticed in the workplace. I was promoted and eventually became the first female supervisor. I thought I was the bee's knees. Career-wise I had made it, or so I thought at the time. I had respect from all my co-workers and I was good at what I did. Probably because I spent so much time at work, my colleagues became my friends.

There were lots of good times, especially working the afternoon shift, which usually ended up as night shift. First of all, anyone who has worked an afternoon shift would know that it usually means working 3 p.m. to 11 p.m. – on paper, yes, but in reality not so much.

Anyway, like most nights, especially using the new super-duper computer to plate machine, there would always be a problem. The plate getting stuck was the usual culprit. Sometimes this would happen half a dozen times throughout the night but, of course, always close to home time. So you would get in this thing, because you could, trying to pull plates out, which sometimes you couldn't even find. It may not sound like fun, but we enjoyed ourselves working together to sort it out. Other such memorable moments included our Christmas parties, which went on from midday till sometimes three o'clock the next morning.

In 2002 I took my annual leave and travelled to Greece. What an experience that was. My time in Greece was spent living with a drug dealer/user. He was more than happy for me to stay, but in meeting him I got the impression there was something not right about him. Boy, was I right about that. By day two of my stay, I couldn't believe my living arrangements.

Given the amount of drugs he had injected into his arm over the years, his brain was so fried that he didn't even know how to run a household. So much so that his mother had put a list together, not only on how to operate the washing machine, but a reminder to buy toilet paper, socks and jocks. Everything we seemed to take for granted was clearly a challenge for him. The bigger surprise was him getting so drunk and stoned that he wouldn't make an appearance for three days. I often thought he was dead, but then pop! There he was, alive and kicking for more of the same. Or the endless drinking and cones made out of coke bottles that would turn the house into a nightclub, where the smoke from the drugs was so thick that you couldn't see from one side of the room to the other. But my personal favourite was the spoons that were left on the bathroom basin; somehow I didn't think they were for eating cereal. His kind offer of sex also didn't go unnoticed either; thank you, but no, thank you! The skinny, unhygienic look wasn't what I was looking for in a man.

The icing on the cake, however, was stealing $50 from my purse. This meant that every time I left the room, I had to now carry my passport and cash with me, even to go to the toilet.

The irony of all this was that next door was the police station. They were completely aware of the situation, but did nothing. I can only assume they, too, were making something on the side. The chief inspector was a pig. He used to check me out like I was a piece of meat, but I had to be polite because, of course, he was also the customs officer. Not being nice to him meant not getting off the island and that wasn't an option.

I did eventually find other living arrangements but also had to be careful about how I left. This guy was very unpredictable, so everything had to be done methodically, perfectly timed so he wouldn't get suspicious. Years later, he was murdered.

The trip to Greece was a diversion from what was going on at work. At the time I thought I had a great job with benefits, but what I came to realise is that nothing lasts forever. I thought I was doing a great job. I was the first female supervisor, after all, and clearly status meant a great deal to me back then. However, if you upset the apple cart, you have to deal with the consequences – something I learnt the hard way.

It was clear that the men, predominantly the sales team, more loosely referred to as the 'untouchables' of the company, did not like being told what to do by a woman. The cracks began to show, and I was slowly pushed out. Their ways of doing this were very subtle but their point wasn't. First I was told that the position was going to be made redundant, but I was not. 'We want you to stay, Vic. You're a good worker.' They must have thought I'd come down in the last shower. I went from being supervisor of the design department to folding bits of paper in the bindery department. Not that working in the bindery was a bad thing; it just wasn't for me. In that workplace, people were not made redundant, but their self-esteem and confidence were.

So what started as a successful career move ended in sickness, where I lost three months of my life. I know that sounds dramatic, but I did get very sick. I ended up with a viral infection which kept me bedridden for a week and with breathing difficulties for close to three months. So take it from me if you're not happy in your job and you think you have no other options, you do: leave! Nothing is worth getting sick over. I remember the last few months; I was too scared to take the risk and leave. I was making myself sick. Even driving into the car park made my stomach churn. I used to feel literally sick, like I wanted to vomit. I was unhappy; they made my life a misery, but still I chose to stay.

Fortunately for me, I had a saving grace – martial arts. Coincidentally, in the same week as I'd started work at the printing place, I also went to get some information about joining a martial arts gym. Who could have known what that would lead to? Not only did it open a door for me professionally as an athlete, where I got to travel the world, but more importantly, it became part of my healing process. The ambiguous art disguised as a sport was a kind of therapy, a therapy that saved my life.

20

Martial arts saved my life – saving grace

When I had started martial arts in Berri, a town fifteen minutes from Barmera, my training was in tae kwon do, specifically rhee tae kwon do. Now it was time to get back into it. I already had a brown belt black tip, so I needed to find a gym where I could achieve my black belt. The plan was to stay just long enough to achieve my black belt. I stayed just over eleven years. Clearly the universe had plans for me. I just didn't know it at the time.

I had been feeling lost, looking for something else, another challenge. Thinking back, it was probably more about fitting in than anything else, but I also enjoyed a challenge. No matter the reason, I turned up. Not sure what to expect, I thought I should begin with kick-boxing. It was the in thing back then. I didn't know too much about it at the time.

Back then, my pain threshold was not as high as it is now, and at one particular training session it showed. Towards the end of the class, we were all asked to line up – God knew what was about to happen. The instructor asked each of us to stick our leg out and, one by one, he kicked us in the thigh – fuck!

When he got to me, the kick dropped me like a sack of potatoes. What the hell was that! I can't ever remember experiencing pain like that, even when I did tae kwon do. While it hurt in that moment, it was the best thing that could have happened. It might sound as though the instructor was crazy, but he wasn't. The method behind the madness was to expose his students to the reality of fighting as a metaphor for life. The point he was making was that no one is going to have mercy on you. Be it on the streets or in anything you do, you have to fight for what you want. Life doesn't give you warning signals. It just throws stuff at you, and you have to learn how to deal with it. This gym was not for the faint-hearted. Not that you had to be a fighter to attend, but you had to have a strong mind. And what better way to get one than through physical pain.

The gym was located in suburban Adelaide, not very far from the printing place. There were only three women when I started. One used to train one-on-one with the instructor. The other mainly looked after the admin side of things, but also trained. Lastly, there was Tania, married and a mother of two. I think she started training when her five-year-old son started. We began going to the gym quite regularly in the mornings, so the instructor decided to train all three of us. That's how the morning classes started. As we kept training, I got to know Tania a little more. She was loud, inappropriate at times, wore the shortest of clothes, lived life to the fullest and trained like a demon. She was also the nicest, most good-hearted person you could ever meet, and she accepted me exactly as I was.

I still found it difficult to form friendships. I just stood in the background and watched. I used to stand and train behind the bags during classes. I was very reserved, which was sometimes mistaken for being a snob or a bitch. Thinking about it now, maybe there was something to that. I wasn't the most approachable person, a hard nut to crack, according to some. It didn't seem to be a problem; I was only going to be there a short time. Preparing for the black belt in tae kwon do was my main concern. I kept to myself and just trained. I didn't talk to anyone unless I knew them, unless it was just to be polite. I never went out of my way.

It was all still very new to me, so my standoffish behaviour may have been misinterpreted as a bad attitude. Unfortunately, this behaviour somehow manifested as something worse as the years progressed. It was definitely noticed in the gym by other students and especially by my instructor. He never told me to my face, not until much later, and neither did they. Perhaps someone should have, but they probably thought it wasn't their place or that I was just unapproachable.

Success in the martial arts helped me overcome these problems. It gave me confidence and a sense of accomplishment, but it was only when I started boxing that I really came into my own.

21

How I found boxing – boxing found me

I think it was close to two years before my instructor gave me any real acknowledgment, suggesting I should get in the ring. Wow! Finally he sees me, I thought. I am not invisible. Getting his approval was really important to me at the time.

I can't remember the exact year I started boxing, maybe 2003, maybe earlier. It became the art I loved most. As you get older, you realise that the art is even more important than the physical side of it. I have such an appreciation for it now. At that stage, all I knew was that, like everything in my life, it was going to be a challenge. Lucky for me, I love challenges. I started attending the classes more frequently. When it came to boxing, I was very curious, but you know what happened to the cat? Thankfully, no one got killed. The only thing I had to get used to was getting hit. Once I did, I really started to enjoy it.

But before any of that, I had to start at step one and learn how to move feet, hands and head, basically learn the steps required to make you a boxer. At the time it wasn't something I aspired to do or be; it just happened. Boxing relied on a lot of agility, flexibility and remaining relaxed, none of which I was familiar with at the time. Most importantly you had to be in the right head space. My advantage, when I think about it now, was my 'wog' head. I didn't like to be beaten at something; I pursued it till I got it. There was no exact Aha moment – oh, that's why I box. It just sort of developed over time. It all just started to fit together and I began to take it seriously. I was able to work harder through the classes because I knew what I was doing. I was able to enjoy it more. I loved how hard the classes were. They forced me to see my own potential, to see what I was made of. Granted that was a small part of it; the public act of getting into the ring and boxing was the other part and I was very surprised to realise that I suffered from performance anxiety.

I was still not the happiest person. In fact, I was quite moody at times. I found the classes difficult, which was no surprise given my negative attitude. This attitude got worse before it got better. One of my many great qualities was that when I was learning something, I felt I had to master it straight away. But when learning martial arts, patience is a virtue. Given my high expectations, taking time to learn something was not going to be easy. That was clearly another lesson I had to learn. Most humans are similar in nature. They are not going to like something if they're not good at it. I think I'm still a little that way now. I get annoyed if I can't do something. It frustrates the hell out of me, but I am getting a lot better. I've learned that you just have to stick it out, be honest with yourself and give it a real go.

It took me a long time to understand the concept of boxing, especially the coordination. For example, when one hand hits, the other defends – two different hand movements, too confusing. Getting hit helps with that; you learn very quickly to keep your hands up. I also found boxing a great catalyst for bringing the emotions to the surface. I'm not exactly sure how to explain this, but it's all about fight or flight. Dedication, hard work, discipline and drive are also necessary, just as they are in the wider world.

What I discovered was, if I could put up with the pain in the ring, and keep coming back, then I could do anything. I don't think I found boxing, I think it found me. When I think about it now, I realise I was very lucky. Boxing really made me stronger and gave my life purpose and meaning. I went to the gym a very angry, unhappy person, but from the time I took up boxing, things began to change.

Stepping into the ring requires commitment. You can't just run away when things get too hard. This can make it either one of the scariest things or the most challenging and exciting things you can do. For me, it was both. Whether you're fighting in front of a crowd of ten or 5,000, the feeling is indescribable. You're excited and nervous all at the same time. Your heart's pumping at a million miles an hour and the adrenalin is in overdrive. You just want it to begin, to feel that first punch, so you know what to expect. I loved that feeling!

It's funny because no matter how many times I stepped into the ring, whether it was for a competition or just for a few rounds of sparring, I felt alive. That's what makes boxing. It's about taking risks. There is, however, the fitness and the skill level required to be any good in the ring. Before learning how to box, I knew nothing about it, but once I started, I found there was a lot to learn. The different combinations, blocks, weaves and ducks – that's what I found most intriguing. It was like playing chess. Boxing requires you to outsmart your opponent. You learn how to counter a move, how to read your opponent and, most important, how to take a punch – much like life. It's all about risk, getting out of your comfort zone, and once you've experienced the ring, there is nothing like it. And you learn about the risks very quickly. I have endured multiple injuries, including a cracked rib, bruised arm, black eyes and a broken nose. I don't regret any of them. Why? For one, it's boxing and it's bound to happen. Number two, I have learnt a lot about myself in the process, about how much I can take.

I think also I did it because in some strange way I felt it defined me. That's who I was and what I did, and so without it, I would go back to being the same old person I was before.

For a long time I was the only female boxing competitor at the gym, so it felt like I always had something to prove. My friends at the gym also liked me in my capacity as a boxer. Not that they liked me any less when I wasn't boxing, but I was the one who would compete, train like a crazy person, and take on whoever wanted to fight, be it female or male. It gave me a sense of purpose, like that was my thing and that's what I was good at.

22

My very first fight – what was I thinking?

The first fight is always the hardest: you just don't know what to expect. And the preparation for something like this is like nothing you could imagine. First of all there are the weight categories. If your instructor tells you to start losing weight even though the fight isn't for a few months, listen to him. Expect the unexpected. Not that I was heavy but I wasn't exactly happy with my weight either. I was around 65 to 68 kilos at the time. So this was the first battle I had to endure, followed by stress and anxiety. Stress and anxiety play an important part when you're trying to lose weight; they don't help. So weighing in at 58 kilos was the hardest thing I had to do. The majority of the weight was coming off but it was those last two kilos that would almost be the death of me.

Why, you might ask, would I put myself through this? I wanted to see if I could do it. I also found it to be one of the best ways to learn about my mental strength. I remember the day before the fight like it was yesterday.

I told my instructor, 'If I can't make the weight, then I won't fight.' Yeah, right, that easy – not!

He told me, 'I don't care what you have to do, but you have to drop the weight, and you are going to fight.'

What do you do with that? Could I run? Should I run? What would you do? It was a battle of the mind, feeling bad if I pulled out, plus guilt, all the hard work, letting my instructor down. Let's be real: who was I kidding? Anyone who knows me knows what I was going to do – fight!

At this point, I think many would've given up; I know I wanted to. Why didn't I? Perhaps I was just crazy. Maybe it was all about pride, because giving up meant I'd have failed. I was hardly eating and I was hitting the sauna – hard. On the final morning before the fight, I put on the stick fighting armour. I had a swig of vodka and then went for a run. Thankfully, the weight came off and I was able to fight. Three kilos in one hour, not recommended without supervision, but losing weight this way is normal for boxers. The weigh-in was on the same night as the fight, which was quite ridiculous to me, but they were the rules. I think it's to do with loading up with carbohydrates before the fight, which would give you more energy and perhaps an unfair advantage. Either way, I had to follow the rules.

The day finally arrived. I was excited and nervous, and also extremely hungry. I had never done anything like it before. My instructor met me at the venue. It was in the rules that the instructor and fighter both be there for the weigh-in. I was certainly curious and nervous about my weight. When preparing for this fight, my instructor had told me that his scales were the ones we had to use; they were the most accurate. So I never bothered using mine. Of course, when I turned up on fight night I had all my fighting gear but forgot to bring my bikini. The bikini was the alternative to bra and knickers, which is what you wear to weigh-in. At this point in time, I didn't care if I weighed in naked, but my instructor did. He told me I'd be fine in jeans and a tank top.

'Are you serious?' I said. There was no way I was going to weigh less than 60 kilos in jeans and a tank top. By this stage, I was shitting myself. I had no more weight to lose.

I stepped onto the scales and I weighed in at 57.5 kilos – what the? That night, after the fight, while I was devouring my chicken parmigiana, my instructor revealed that he had adjusted the scales to show my weight as being heavier than it was. A@#hole! I thought at the time, and I told him so. It was one of the methods of his madness I was talking about and it's all to do with the psychology.

I guess he thought that if I knew I had three or four kilos to play with, I probably would have eaten something and undone all my hard work. His way kept you on your toes, and on target weight. It also taught me how to read my own body, to know what I could and could not do – another lesson from my infamous instructor.

I fought but I lost, which is not unexpected on your first fight. I had it video-recorded. No matter how badly you think you fought and even though you never want to repeat the fight again, you're always curious about your performance. After that first experience, I discovered it's never about the fight – anyone can learn to fight. It's about how much you're willing sacrifice to reach your goal. How far will you go? And according to my sister, at the time I looked like a ghost, so obviously I went pretty far. Wouldn't you, for something you wanted so badly?

Boxing is a sport where you learn a lot about yourself. It forces you to confront your emotions, where your responses are fight or flight. It's just you and your opponent, who basically wants to knock your head off. At the same time, it's the most invigorating, challenging, adrenalin-based battle of your life. I may have lost that fight, but I learnt something about myself. I felt invincible. I felt like I could do anything. I still believe that today.

One of my favourite boxing movies is *Million Dollar Baby* – surprise, surprise. It was Morgan Freeman's character who said it best: 'The magic of boxing is risking everything for a dream that no one sees but you.' That says it all.

People often ask me why I would put myself through that, knowing I'm going to get hurt. You know what I say? Because I know I am probably going to get hurt and that's okay.

What does it feel like to get hit? It's hard for me to remember. Sounds crazy, I know, but it's true. Every time you get into the ring, it's guaranteed you will get hit, even if you're a good boxer. There's no getting out of it. The only word I can use to describe it is shock. You don't actually feel the pain; it's the shock that has more of an effect. The interesting thing about getting hit is that you don't actually see it coming, because obviously you'd get out the way.

The very first time you get hit, you experience many emotions – the first being fear, anxiety – and you tend to start breathing very quickly, almost like you're hyperventilating. The body tenses up, so that everything you do feels like you're in slow motion. Your punches feel very slow. The reaction you have also depends on where you get hit. Obviously getting hit in the face will give you the biggest shock. Your face goes numb and you just freeze. The best way to deal with getting hit is to just keep getting hit. There is no magic trick. It's like falling off a bike and hurting yourself. You just have to get back on and keep going. The more conditioned you become to it, the less effect it will have.

The body shots are a little different. They really hurt, especially if you get hit in the liver, spleen or solar plexus. All those hits make you winded, so you feel like you can't breathe. The best advice I can give is just compose yourself the best you can and keep going. A fighter's normal reaction after getting hit is to hit back – and hard. An inexperienced fighter's reaction is to run, cover up or just hit hard as soon as the first round begins, avoiding getting hit at all, neither of which is a good idea. The fear and anxiety do subside. The more you get hit, the better equipped you become to deal with it. Unfortunately, there is no timeline. It's different for everyone.

By that stage, I was somewhat used to getting hit but, as a reminder, I liked sparring with my instructor. If you can take his hits, you can take anything. The first round is always the hardest. As I've said, the worst thing about getting hit is that you don't know when it's coming. You try and prepare yourself mentally, but before you know it, you're hit!

This is going to sound crazy, but if it came down to a choice about where I would rather get hit, it would be the head. The liver shot is the most excruciating pain you can ever experience. It's like someone shoved a knife into your liver. It's a really sharp pain. You actually feel like your liver is going to come out of your bum. The recovery period from a hit to the liver takes longer than one to the head. In this, it's very similar to stick fighting. The shots to your fingers, especially your thumb, or a hit to the shoulder, hurt more than a hit to the head. You think all that protection would help ease the pain, but it doesn't.

There is a moment, though, when you accept the hit without thinking which is really quite liberating and powerful. For example, you get a hook to the head; you acknowledge the hit, process the power of the hit, and continue boxing. Of course, this all has to happen in a matter of seconds, otherwise you get hit again. What also happens when you counter a punch is that you're no longer afraid. You're rattled, but you shake it off and keep fighting.

23

The fight that never happened – my poor rib!

You can't just stop at just one fight, so straight after the first one, there was going be a second. I was pretty fit at that stage and prepared, so why not? Unfortunately, it didn't happen.

It was a Tuesday morning and the fight was on the Friday night, so there was still a bit of preparation to do. My instructor decided we needed to spar. Sparring is fighting but not in a competitive sense. He set the clock for three-minute rounds, nothing new, and I had done this before – but not like this. I knew it was going to be long and painful; what I didn't count on was getting the caning of my life. Don't get me wrong, though; he doesn't do this for the pleasure of it. It's all about teaching. Basically it forced me to ask myself how much I really wanted to do it. That's what it's all about, especially if you've already fought in the ring.

During one of the rounds, I looked at the clock and saw Round 11. I remember thinking, just one more round to go. Like so many times before, I was wrong. Boy, was I wrong. We were going the full twenty rounds. What we were doing was probably not considered boxing by normal standards. It's actually what he liked to call education. Basically he did it to see what I was made of. By Round 16, I wanted to run for my life. I was on all fours, blood gushing out my nose, and had a cracked rib, which I didn't know at the time. What was I thinking? Was I so desperate to prove to myself and others that I could handle anything, even if it meant getting injured? Clearly I was, despite the circumstances. Still I continued. I figured if I'd survived sixteen rounds, what were four more?

After that education, there were a couple of people not happy with my instructor, but I didn't blame him for any of my injuries. This is it: if you're going to commit yourself in the ring, then you just have to take whatever comes your way. Of course, he felt bad, but that was his method. He wanted me to understand that if that's really what I wanted to do, that's what it was going to be like. Honestly, I would do it all again.

It's really scary when you get in the ring with him. It's especially scary when it's been a while and you've forgotten what one of his punches feels like. At the same time, it's exhilarating. In order to understand it, you have to relate to it; and the only way to relate to it is by doing it.

I finished the sparring session but, with a cracked rib, I wasn't fit to fight. But this didn't stop me from entering the City to Bay run, which I'd put my name down for weeks earlier.

I really wanted to prove to myself that I could do it. I wanted to prove it to my instructor as well. Many thought I was crazy and maybe I was, but whatever the reason, I still did it. I think if I gave up, it would've felt like I was giving up on myself. I had convinced myself that causing more injury was never an issue. I trained for it and I was still going to do it. I wasn't going to let an injury stop me. Race day, I took to the track and, an hour and eight minutes later, I finished the race.

24

An unorthodox instructor – do you have what it takes?

Yelling was a big part of my instructor's unorthodox methods, but what coach or instructor doesn't yell? His yelling gave me anxiety attacks, which resulted in tears most of the time, but was it that my anxiety already existed and only revealed itself when I was pushed? While it may seem cruel from the outside, his sole objective was to get me out of my comfort zone, and rightfully so. You know the saying 'You can lead a horse to water but you can't make them drink' – well, he could. The slow, soft approach did not exist. Fear, what fear? He had this ability to see straight through us. He would find our fears and drive them out, so eventually we feared nothing. While this sounds very harsh, his methods were successful. Don't get me wrong, I didn't always agree with his ways. There were times when I was furious with him. But what student doesn't hate their instructor at times? Clearly, it was what I needed. Granted it wasn't for everyone, but it was right for me.

My training began with the twelve o'clock boxing class. It was non-contact, more technical. I remember he used to tease me about my style, not because I didn't know what I was doing, but more because the technique wouldn't have worked in boxing. I was still using my tae kwon do technique, punching from the hip, instead of the boxing technique, hands up, punching from the chin. The difference: with the first you would end up lying horizontal on the floor, as I later discovered.

My instructor was a difficult man to get to know, but it wasn't my job to get to know him. It was his job to get to know me and that's exactly what he did. He always said his job was to see the potential in people that they don't see in themselves. But first of all, you had to earn his respect. I don't think he ever said more than ten words to me in a conversation. Well, not until training began for the 2005 World Stick Fighting competition.

In 2005 we were told the United States was going to hold the first World Stick Fighting Championship. The training was hard and my instructor was equally hard. He was very demanding and made us spend long hours practising stick fighting drills. I found it extremely difficult and there were times when I felt like he didn't really want to try and help me. Maybe I should have talked to him about it; maybe he should have approached me; but none of those things happened. We just continued until it didn't matter any more. The only thing I could think was that maybe he was pissed that I had made my decision to compete at the eleventh hour. Either way, I hated him for it. But really, maybe it was myself I hated more. I remember thinking I already had people making me feel bad at work. I didn't need this shit on top of that. Especially in this place, the place I once considered my home, my saving grace. I felt like I had nowhere else to go, no place where I could feel or be myself.

While my instructor would never discourage anyone from having a go, I actually wish he'd stopped me from entering the World Stick Fighting Competition in 2005. Who was I kidding? I wasn't ready. I should have just stayed home. I was using the competition to run away from my problems instead of dealing with them head on. Maybe what I thought about him was really about me. I wanted so much to be a part of something, and when I felt he wasn't helping me, it was disappointment all over again.

Irrespective of the lead-up, I went to the gym and continued training. Ultimately, I went to the competition, spent thousands of dollars, had one fight and lost – end of story.

Of course, I went back. But that was after a significant time away taking time to concentrate on other things like my work and to figure out what I really wanted. During that time, I felt like I was under a lot of pressure from work as well as from my instructor, and I just needed a break. When I returned to fighting, I was focused and ready to conquer the world, or at least the stick fighting world.

25

Becoming a personal trainer – the passion begins here

Most of 2006 was spent working. After finally making the decision to leave the printing place – which, by the way, was the best decision I ever made – I got a new job working as a personal trainer. I threw myself into it hard – maybe too hard. It didn't take long to get busy, so busy that I spent most of my time working and not much time training. That was the sacrifice which had to be made in order to make a living. At first, I worked at four different gyms. Eventually, four turned into three and then they finally turned into one. I was good at my job and possibly a little cocky. I was averaging forty sessions a week and, as a trainer, that's the sort of target you want to be reaching. But it didn't take long before I started to get angry, tired, exhausted and frustrated. Realistically, no trainer could manage those hours, not even me, the indestructible. As I started caring less, the clients started to drop off. I was working a lot of hours and they were taking their toll.

    I didn't realise at the time, but it's amazing how the universe gives you what you want, even when you don't ask for it. Obviously the message I was sending out was 'I don't want to do this any more. I'm too tired. I need a break.' Be careful what you wish for, because my prayers were answered. Whatever I wished for started to happen. The first was the loss of hours, but losing hours meant losing money, which of course brought on more stress – just what I needed, not. I guess that's when I started to feel depressed again. I was looking for something else, but what? If only there was an easy answer to that question.

Around 2006 I applied for a full-time supervising position. It was something I had no doubts about. I could do the job and I could do it well.

So after changing to a full-time position at work, I was ready to go back to the gym. I started going a little more regularly towards the end of 2006. I also decided that if I was going to go back, I wanted to work towards something – I was going to take my martial arts as far as I could go.

26

My second degree grading – another stripe to my belt

Looking up at my office wall, I have my martial arts certificates staring back at me. I was first graded in 2003, receiving a black belt in karate. A first and second degree black belt followed. In 2005 I was graded to first degree black belt in Doce Pares Eskrima (stick fighting), followed by the second and third degrees. Martial art degrees follow a similar format to university degrees. A black belt is equivalent to a bachelor's degree and the dans or first degree and so on is the same as an honours or masters degree. My run in the martial arts ended with a second degree in karate and fourth degree in Doce Pares Eskrima.

I remember my first grading for karate, having to go through all the kartas for the exam. Kartas are a combination of moves, each karta having 20, 30 or 40 moves. I did this first grading with another girl and we stuffed up due to nerves. As punishment, our instructor made us do 100 push-ups and start again. If 100 push-ups sound like a lot, he made young kids do the same thing, especially if they were going for their black belt. He also had us breaking a few tiles with just a punch. Once again, when you're doing something like that, you never think about injury – well, I never did. The higher the grade you're trying to achieve, the more tiles you have to break.

I have so many memories of my gradings. The most memorable was for my second degree black belt in Doce Pares Eskrima. I was nowhere near ready – so many things to remember – but my instructor, being the person he was, didn't care, and I don't mean that in a bad way.

He knew I could do it, but I doubted myself and he could see that. I tried to explain time and time again that I wasn't ready, but he chose to ignore me. In martial arts, especially grading, if your instructor tells you that you're ready to grade, you grade, no ifs or buts.

I'd been training for about two months when he said to me, 'You're going to grade next week.'

I said, 'What! But I'm not ready!' Having a negative attitude at the gym is a big no-no. You can only imagine the reaction I got, so I graded.

The other problem with a negative attitude is that you've already convinced yourself that you can't do something. I was a master at that.

Working full-time, I couldn't get to the gym as often as I wanted or needed to, and by the time Friday night came – we were grading Saturday – scared was an understatement. When it comes to an exam, I can and will do it successfully as long as you don't call it an exam, assessment or test. I think it's all in the name.

Saturday arrived and there were only two of us being graded. I was nervous, and with the nerves came errors, and a lot of them. The errors occurred in every facet of the grading. I was getting crucified. He knew it was the nerves, but he also knew how to get to me. I'm not sure if there were tears, but I am sure I wanted to cry. First part, second part, third part, then came the sparring; that was the best bit. We had to spar with three masters plus with the other student grading.

Stick fighting is exactly what the name suggests: you hit and get hit with a stick made of cane, and it hurts – it hurts a lot. When getting hit with the stick, especially for the first time, you feel a stinging sensation, but then it passes. You wear headgear which is padded on the side and the back but has a cage built in the front of it, so you can still see without getting seriously hurt. In this case, we did it without armour and without the stick being taped up. Each round went for two or three minutes. The first round was with a visiting master from a different school. He was a little kinder than the other two.

I was glad that I sparred with the visiting master first. It was preparation for the pain I was going to receive from my instructor. The second session was with a master who also taught at the gym and, last but not least, was a session with my instructor. While the hits were not hard, they were certainly on target. By the end of it, I had little red marks all over the exposed parts of my body, on my stomach, arms, legs, above the knee. No place was safe – other than the chest. At that moment, I was glad to be female; otherwise I would've had all these marks across my chest as well.

I was proud of my achievement. It's not every day that you can say you sparred with three masters under the same roof. The grading went for a couple of hours, very intense, but well worth it.

We put our minds and bodies through such stress each and every day; we just have nothing to show for it. At least with this kind of training, you know what to expect; there are no surprises. Well, there are a few, but once you get that first initial hit, that's it, you're ready. The whole point is to strengthen your mind. If you can take the physical pain, you can train your mind to take other pain.

27

It's all in your head – help comes whether you like it or not

It seemed that, having achieved some success in my life, my confidence began to grow and strengthen. I started to see more of what was going on outside myself and was no longer confined in my own little bubble. I began to see that other people also had their problems.

It was while I was training for the Stick Fighting World Titles in Jakarta that I met Melissa. It's hard to believe now, but I never had much patience with kids, especially teenagers. So imagine my surprise when this young kid came into my life, changing my whole perspective on kids. We didn't have a lot to do with each other to begin with, until we travelled to Wollongong, and then there began this great friendship. I used to take her home from training, and we'd catch up for coffee, or go to the movies. She'd also text me in the middle of the night just randomly. Teenagers!

Melissa hadn't lived the easiest life and basically in my head I wanted to save her. Or was it me I was trying to save? This kid was such a challenge. She had built a wall around herself that you needed a sledgehammer to get through. I felt privileged that she confided in me. The irony was that she wore her heart on her sleeve, just like me. That's probably what drew her to me in the first place. We developed a really great bond. She became like a little sister. We'd talk about everything – well, everything she wanted to talk about. I could see she was starting to trust me. I would have done anything for that kid. Helping her made me realise the joy of helping other people, especially young people.

I decided to study psychology. But before that, I realised I needed to seek therapy for myself. I knew had a lot of work to do on my own feelings and attitudes and trying to fix them on my own was no longer an option. So rather than trying to use the study of psychology as my quick fix, as so many do, I chose to pick up the phone.

It was not the first time I had picked up the phone. It was, however, the first time I had actually dialled the number, spoken to the receptionist and made the appointment. It no longer felt like a choice, but more like something I had to do. If I wanted to help others, I had to help myself first.

Today I believe it was the combination of my instructor's 'never give up' attitude and that beautiful little kid, who is now in her twenties, that led me to the psychologist's chair. She helped me change into a person who no longer cared only about herself, but was more concerned with other people. Maybe I was always that way but didn't allow myself to show it.

Being Greek doesn't only bring tradition, big families and overprotective parents; it also brings a Greek's worst enemy – pride. Having a ridiculous amount of pride prevents us from asking for help. It is also a sign of weakness, or is it? Well, that's what I was led to believe. Seeking therapy is taboo, especially when you come from a European background, most specifically Greek, and live in a country town. You don't need help; you're just having a bad day. If I cry, I'm weak. If I discuss my emotions, I'm weak. What will people say?

We never spoke about our emotions at home. There was no sitting at the kitchen table talking about our problems. It was just not something my family did. For close to thirty years, I had kept my emotions locked in, which made me a very angry person. I think there was a time when I was suffering depression. I felt it inside, in my heart, in my head, but at the time I couldn't explain it. I went to my doctor and told him I needed to see someone but instead of helping me, he made feel worse. He told me, 'There's nothing wrong with you, you'll be fine' – but I wasn't. His attitude was no surprise. He was an old-school Greek doctor after all, and clearly not a very smart one. So I just kept going the same way. The anger was there all the time. My attitude sucked. In fact, there was a year there when I was without friends and couldn't work out why. It was obviously them, not me, who had the problem.

I know it sounds like I blame a lot on my Greek heritage, but at the time who or what else could I have blamed it on? Me? Anyway, as the gods or the universe would have it, I was going to get the help I needed whether I wanted it or not. Remember what I said about the universe?

One of my personal training clients was a psychologist. I was training him and his wife at least four or five times a week and this gave me the opportunity to ask a couple of questions – like they couldn't see straight through that. They had me worked out as soon as I walked through the door. They knew me better than I knew myself, not that that was hard.

There were so many times that I wanted to make an appointment, so many arguments I had in my head. I always managed to convince myself I was 'fine' which is an acronym of fucked, insane, neurotic and emotional. Oh yeah, I was definitely fine.

Finally I bit the bullet and went for my first session. It was nothing like I expected. Upon arrival, he asked me to sit down, offered me a drink and tried to make me feel as comfortable as possible. He then asked me about my family and, even worse, about myself. It was at that point that I brought out reinforcements – food, or more specifically an apple, so I could avoid crying.

Talk about getting out of my comfort zone, it was something I would never had done a few years ago and I am so proud that I did. My psychologist described me as an emotional time bomb.

How does therapy actually work? I can only tell you from my experience. We started with a few sessions bunched together, then slowly cut them down to fortnightly, then monthly, and then I was given homework. He taught me how to breathe, not in the literal sense, but to bring all the negative thoughts that I had buried back to the surface and release them. That helped me. I noticed small changes, but changes nonetheless. I had about five sessions, and am happy to admit that whenever I feel like I can't solve something, I go again. I recommend this to anyone who feels like the walls are crashing down around them or even if they just need to chat to someone.

During my time with the psychologist, maybe during the second or third session, I explained how I struggled when I got in the ring, just minutes before a fight. Struggle was an understatement. He explained that its technical term is performance anxiety, or stage fright, and basically it's the fear of being the centre of attention. The treatment involved hypnosis, having me going under, imagining myself entering the ring, the crowd of people, explaining what I see, how I should be feeling.

The timing couldn't have been better, given I had the World Stick Fighting titles coming up. Was I sure it was going to work? I had no idea, but I had to try something.

The sessions, taught me a lot about myself. So as a reminder, should I ever need one, I decided to write myself a letter, not because I was crazy, but just as a reminder that everything was going to be okay:

Dear Vickie,
While I know you say you have no regrets, I know you do, and if you knew then what you know now, things would've been very different. Now you're older and wiser and deserve all the good things. Stop obsessing about the things that don't matter and concentrate on the things that do.

You are beautiful and smart and have a kick-arse body to boot. I know you want the fairy tale, but wishing it won't make it happen. Be patient and love yourself first and foremost, and the rest will follow.

Of course there are some things we can't control but save it for the big things. Getting hurt is part of life. Fall in love, make mistakes, enjoy the journey, and learn from it.

Think intelligently and not emotionally – there will always be a time and place for that – and finally, laugh as much as you can. Take a little bit from everyone and make it your own.

There is a reason why the universe threw a martial arts instructor, three psychologists and certain friends at you, so you could learn how to ask for help, but mainly just to learn. Some of these people will be forever and some temporary, but don't feel bad if they leave; just know that you have taken what you have needed from them, as they have taken from you. For those who have stayed, you may still be teaching them or them you. Either way, have confidence in yourself, accept all your faults and qualities, and most importantly stay true to who you are.

You have learnt so much about yourself; don't let self-doubt pull you back in. Life is very much like fighting in the ring, and you have never backed down from a fight despite a cracked rib, a broken finger and a broken nose, so enjoy the ride.

Love Vickie x

28

World titles Jakarta 2007 – one moment in time

How do you describe a moment? Is it a single, life-changing event? Or is it a catalyst for one major event? Lyrics of a song have a great way of describing a feeling or an emotion that we sometimes cannot put into words. Whitney Houston's song 'One Moment in Time' describes the feeling perfectly:

> One moment in time, when I'm more than I thought I could be,
> when all of my dreams are a heartbeat away
> and the answers are all up to me.

This song talks about that one moment when, by putting in the hard work, you can achieve anything you want. Life presents you with an opportunity, and you don't want to waste it. That's how I felt when my instructor told me that I would be a formidable opponent, a potential contender for gold or silver at the 2007 World Stick Fighting tournament in Jakarta.

At the time, it was important to me to achieve something I never thought I could. Granted everyone is different and we are all driven by different forces. I am not the same person I was back then, but I think it's important to reflect on moments like these and be grateful. It's also important not to forget the people who helped you get there. This was just one moment out of so many which instilled my confidence to do well. But the training is where it all began.

I took stick fighting classes after we got back from the USA, mainly to improve my technique and skill, which had been non-existent at the USA comps. I had struggled with stick fighting before, so I wanted to excel in it. I didn't want to be just good at something; I wanted to be great. At the time, it seemed like the only way. I was working full-time but I really wanted to compete, so I trained several hours a day, five days a week. A couple of the guys used to stay back and train with me on Thursday nights, giving me a few rounds each. Once my instructor saw my dedication, he made the whole team stay back and do a few rounds with me. I remember one night he asked one of the team members how many rounds he thought I should do. He replied in his Polish accent, 'Eight rounds, three minutes each round' – thanks for that!

Preparation is the part of the competition I enjoy the most, pushing myself to a level I never thought I could reach. That's what I did. That's what we all did. Once we achieved it, the fight was the easy part. We had the fitness; we had the skill and technique; all we had to do was fight well – but that bit was up to us. Basically it comes down to how badly you want something. If you want it badly enough, you can achieve it. You can achieve anything. I mean, look at me! In my wildest dreams, I couldn't have imagined winning in any sport, especially in a world title tournament, but for me, my first bout was my first win.

We were probably weeks away from the world titles and training became a lot more specific. The baseball bat was used for the Amarra or warm-up drills, to improve wrist flexibility. Then a lighter stick was used for the practical drills, for building speed. For that one hour, the boxing bag became my opponent, so a lot of time was spent hitting the bag with different strikes.

The more hitting I did, the more the skin between my thumb and index finger became red and bloody. It stung and it bloody hurt, but I just had to keep going. It did eventually heal and become hard, but going without gloves was for training purposes only. When we were competing, we always wore gloves; otherwise there would have been a lot of broken fingers. The training sessions varied: sometimes I would wear the helmet and gloves; other days it was just bare skin and the stick.

This particular day was like any other training session. It was about nine o'clock on a Tuesday morning and I was working through my drills as normal. I overheard my instructor telling the other master how hard I'd been training. He'd noticed I was bleeding but was impressed that I never stopped training. He also said I had a chance of winning silver or gold. I never expected to hear that. That was the moment when everything I'd worked for came to life. It was really important to me, to prove to him that I could do it, and that he finally saw it. His approval meant a lot to me during that part of my life. I needed to be good at something and finally I was. My skill level went from being mediocre to silver and gold level.

Our private classes were based on the technique and skills of stick fighting. I thought it would help me feel less inadequate, but I found the classes extremely difficult and couldn't keep up. Whether the instructor was going too fast or my brain was going too slow, I'm not sure. But he didn't like it when I fell behind, not because he thought I couldn't do it, but because he wanted me to try harder. Yes, I got yelled at, and yes, I was made to feel like crap, but maybe I allowed myself to feel that way. No one can make you feel a particular way. It's up to you how you react.

Sometimes the yelling is actually what you need, to make you feel alive, to wake you up and make you want to fight for something. Clearly the man knew me better than I knew myself. The yelling and the put-downs were not meant to make me feel bad; they were designed to make me step it up and fight.

Granted this form of training isn't for everyone. There were definitely times when I wanted to crawl under a rock or go into the foetal position, but I didn't. I stayed, I fought, and eleven years later I was still there, so he must have been doing something right. The thing about my instructor was that he expected people to put in the work. We had to be dedicated, not just half-arsed dedicated. As soon as he saw that I was willing to put in the work, his respect for me grew. And once I realised what I had to do, I got his help in return.

As we worked together in preparation for the championships, our relationship started to change. Our conversations became not only about training but about life. And so it began – discussions about situations, people, our own problems, and slowly, slowly, we gained a mutual respect for each other. He would give advice and I would listen, and vice versa. What once began as instructor and student relationship was developing into a friendship. He was never one to take advantage of his status in the martial arts world. We had mutual respect and because of that, he often felt free to say whatever he wanted. It sometimes made me want to slap him, when he stepped over the mark just that little bit – the whole gym didn't need to know about my love life, or lack of one. I guess we can call it a 'caring moment'.

Although his training methods were unorthodox, there was something about them that made me want to stay. One of my first memories of him was when we were doing a karate class outside in the rain. It was not just a little shower; it was full-blown wind and rain. I remember thinking, is this guy insane? Whether he was or wasn't, I did the class anyway. In fact, now I enjoy training in the rain. There's something refreshing about it, almost like a freedom, a letting go.

I guess at this point people might wonder what possessed me to stick around. I had seen people come and go, and it seemed that only the strong survived. It certainly wasn't for the faint-hearted. But there was something about it; I can't quite put it into words, only to say that it made me feel alive. I wanted to be strong, physically and especially mentally. The training was never only about the training. It was about pushing myself, getting out of my comfort zone.

Finally the day arrived. We got to the stadium really early, only to learn that the men were going to fight the full three days of the tournament, because there were more male competitors, and the women would only fight on the second and third days. It was actually a relief to know I had one more day to prepare myself – mentally, that is.

Day two couldn't come quickly enough. I felt prepared and so pumped, there were no nerves or anxiety. I couldn't wait to fight. My only goal at that point was to win my first fight; anything after that was just a bonus. I didn't care about silver or gold. I just wanted to get through the first round.

Each round was one minute, one very fast minute. First, second, third round, and then I was told it was a draw! I couldn't believe it. A draw means that you have to go for a fourth round. By the end of the first round, you're exhausted. Everything affects you on the first round, your nerves and your fitness, so you can imagine the third! The whistle blew and I went my absolute hardest. I put everything into that round and a minute later, it ended.

The helmets were off. We were both standing in the ring with the referee, waiting for the final count from the judges. He was holding each of our hands. I was nervous. I began to pray, asking God for a win, and finally my hand was lifted. I couldn't believe it. My prayers had been answered. I wanted to cry, but I just moved around the ring pumping my fist through the air. I'd done it! It didn't matter that it was my first fight in the competition. I didn't care how many I won after that.

The remaining fights were just a blur. I fought, I won. I think I had about fourteen fights over the remaining two days and I won most of them. I was exhausted, but it was so worth it. My instructor was right. I did have a good chance for silver or gold. I finished up with two silver medals and a bronze. What a day! What a moment!

29

Philippines 2008 – the Gathering

In March 2008, I attended the Gathering in the Philippines, a martial arts seminar held over three days. It included various martial arts experts from many different countries, each sharing their knowledge, skills and wisdom with students from around the world. During that time I got to meet some of these experts, and what an honour it was. They were all very humble and happy to share their experiences with like-minded students like myself.

The days started at 9 a.m. and went till about 4.30 p.m. The building was not too far from our hotel, but with the ten or more students we had from our gym, we needed to hire a bus. The temperature in the Philippines is quite humid, especially in March, and the location where the seminar was held was not air-conditioned, so there were some unwell, dehydrated students. I managed to survive all three days, surprisingly, considering I celebrated my birthday the night before we arrived.

As all the drills were partner drills, we always had to work with a partner. The partners were not necessarily people we knew, same gender or people we necessarily liked, for that matter.

Each instructor was skilled in their individual martial art, which meant that we were able to learn and experience a variety of martial arts, including disarming weapons. They were tiring days but very fulfilling, and the knowledge that we walked away with was world-renowned.

On the third day, we attended the first Hall of Fame dinner. The men were dressed in white shirts and black slacks and the women had free choice. I wore a red and black halter neck dress, with my hair down, and a small-heeled shoe.

The medals were given out first. As our names were called, we walked up to the stage. I collected two silver medals and a bronze. Then, like everyone else, after I had received my medals, I followed the tradition of approaching the Supreme Grandmaster, taking his hand and bowing down to it as a sign of respect and gratitude.

Once all the medals had been presented, it was time for the awards. I received the award for most notable competitor of the year. It was a statue of a Filipino figure holding two sticks. Winning the award was the equivalent of winning a Logie in the martial arts world.

What an incredible few days!

30

Making new friends – having my back!

By now I was more open to making new friends. It was around this time that I met two of my good friends, Nadia and Vicki.

Nadia and I became friends the old-fashioned way, working for the same company. Ironically, we became better friends after she left in 2008. She would hate me writing about her, but she was such a significant person in my journey. How did we become friends? It was one of the most asked questions when people found out we were friends. We were nothing alike; we were chalk and cheese, oil and water; basically, we agreed on nothing, but could talk for ages. That's what made the friendship so unique. Nadia was one of those people who could do anything she put her mind to. She had the ability to learn something and learn it extremely well. She was nine years younger than me, but what she lacked in age she made up for in wisdom and despite the age gap there were days when I felt like the younger one.

I learnt so much from Nadia. The most important thing she taught me was processing. What does that mean? Most Europeans tend to react with their heart rather than their head, which was one of the things I used to do. Rather than reacting, I have learnt to take a moment, or moments depending on the situation, think, and then respond. Through my eleven years of training and competing, Nadia was one of my biggest supporters – and she still is.

My friendship with Vicki was also slow starting, but I guess it's also the reason it's still going strong. She initially came to me for training once a week. After the training ended, we spoke maybe twice or three times a year. It only really changed around 2010. We discovered that we had the Riverland in common. She, too, was raised there but moved to Adelaide as a young child. She was a mother of two and ridiculously academic, with three or four university degrees on her wall. She also had an amazing ability to keep moving forward no matter what was in her way, a trait she shared with Nadia. Vicki became the Christina Yang to my Meredith Grey, 'my person'. If you know the show, you'll know what I am talking about.

It was a good time in my life. I discovered that I didn't have to prove myself to be a good friend. I didn't have to go above and beyond; I could just be me. I think it was the first time I began to like myself again.

31

Always the underdog, but who's complaining? – nothing's worth doing if it comes easy

After we returned from the Philippines, I had another boxing match in Wollongong. I remember it because I fought with a fractured finger, which was a stupid accident that happened while I was training one of my clients. I was still a little jet-lagged but thought I'd be okay. Our sessions involved boxing and I decided to go without the focus mitts. As my client punched, I felt a funny sensation in my right index finger. Taking a look, I saw that it was bent in the opposite direction. I figured it was dislocated. It didn't look good at all. The client was more freaked out than I was, especially as she watched me put it back. I had often seen my instructor put fingers, shoulders and noses, including mine, back in their rightful places. I knew I could do the same. I pulled the finger to put it back into its normal position, but nothing changed. I tried a second time and that time, thank God, it worked.

On the way to the hospital, my finger was bleeding and I had a cloth wrapped around it. I found out later from the surgeon that I had damaged my tendon. But I could still bend my finger and that was the main thing. Lucky it was my right finger and not the left. I'm left-handed and the left hand was my jabbing hand, the hand that can win you fights. Obviously I couldn't use my right hand for a while. I still had the stitches in my finger.

Once the stitches came out, I went back to using the right hand again. It was still quite painful, especially when my instructor would make me use it by hitting the focus mitts. It sounds cruel, but it was necessary. Once the first few hits were out of the way and the finger started to warm up, the pain went away. The fight had already been set up so I couldn't really back out, nor did I want to.

At that point in my life it still mattered what people thought, especially my instructor. Also I did really want to fight. A part of me loved being the underdog, and having injuries made it all that more challenging. Maybe subconsciously it was also a good excuse if I lost.

The finger had not recovered fully, but that didn't matter; the main thing was that I fought. There were supposed to be two of us girls going to the tournament. However, the other girl pulled out and, coincidentally, so did my opponent. At least the swap was going to be easy. I was surprisingly relaxed when we got to the venue. In fact, a few people came up to me and commented on how relaxed I looked. Finally, I thought, I've beaten whatever it was, the craziness and the anxiety that had taken me hostage all these years was gone – wrong!

It happened as I was waiting for my turn to fight. I was just sitting there, listening to music, relaxing, not really thinking about anything in particular, when one of the promoters came in and told me that my fight had been pushed forward. Someone hadn't turned up. Shit! In a matter of seconds the anxiety came back, this time with a vengeance. I felt numb all over. My heart was beating loudly, almost jumping out of my chest.

My instructor then came in, guns blazing. 'Hurry up, get ready, put your gloves on and start warming up.'

As I began hitting those focus mitts, everything felt like it was happening in slow motion. I knew it was the performance anxiety happening again, but I could do nothing to stop it.

My name was announced, and I started to walk into the stadium, aware that there were probably about 5,000 people watching. The bell rang for the first round. I had no chance; there were punches being thrown everywhere, but not by me. My opponent was quite a solid girl, I think a bit heavier than 60 kilos. She was from a Kiwi background and could certainly pack a punch. It felt like she was playing cymbals with my head! I couldn't wait for the bell to ring to end the round, not because I was scared, but so that I could compose myself and focus.

The round ended and my instructor told me, 'She wants a war, so you're going to have to give her a war, Vick' – and that I did.

I think in some strange way I loved being the underdog. Unless I pulled out a miracle, like a knockout, and not my own, there was no way I was going to win.

Round two began and with everything I had I threw a right upper cut, a left hook and a straight right, hoping to drop her. Unfortunately, I was unsuccessful. It didn't matter, though. In that short amount of time, all my inhibitions disappeared and I felt normal again. Those three punches were premeditated. I had a plan and whether it worked or not didn't matter.

There were tears after the fight; that was to be expected. Boxing is an emotional sport. It has a funny way of bringing your emotions to the surface. I was so disappointed, but in hindsight it was one of the best fights I could have hoped for.

32

Gold in New Zealand 2008
– remaining humble

The 2008 Pan Pacific Stick Fighting Competition was held in New Zealand. At first I wasn't sure I wanted to go through it all again. Endless hours of training, watching my weight, potentially no life – I was over it! It was all getting a little tiresome, and it showed in the training, because it was hurting much more than usual. If I was going to pull out, I wanted to be sure it was what I really wanted to do. I knew I couldn't go back. I thought about it a lot, weighed up the pros and cons and asked myself what was really important. Did I really want to do it? Or was I doing it to please other people?

I came to the realisation that it was actually work that was pulling me down, not the training. Once I realised that, my attitude changed. I was on fire. It was an opportunity to win gold! I never told anyone I wanted to; it was my little secret. My instructor always told us not to get lost in winning, otherwise you forget about the fight.

When preparing for a fight or even just in training, you should always expect to get hurt. I think that's part of the attraction. At the end of the day I'm a big believer in the saying 'What doesn't kill you makes you stronger.' I remember one Thursday night training session, I was going pretty hard with my instructor and I got quite a battering. My left arm was in excruciating pain, as were my hand and finger and especially my shoulder. My instructor has the best shoulder shot. He hits you between the bone and the soft bit, basically where the nerve is. You don't really feel it until you stop and the body has time to cool down. Then the pain generates from your arm to the rest of your body, especially your neck and head.

I was a bit nervous approaching Saturday afternoon's training session. I could tell that my arm was not going to do what I wanted it to do. Knowing all that, I still went, thinking I might get some sympathy just for showing up. Who was I kidding? He totally lost it, because I wasn't doing what I was supposed to be doing. In that one instant, the anxiety crept back into my head. I could feel myself starting to hyperventilate, but managed to control it. I had to suck it up and worry about the pain later. It's really quite amazing what a big part your mind plays in the recovery. At first it really hurt, but as I kept going it wasn't that bad. He is quite experienced when it comes to injuries. He knew exactly what he was doing when he told me to continue fighting, because a lot of the time it's your mind that's stopping you, not the injury.

After training I think he did feel bad, because he agreed to massage the bruising out of my shoulder, using the Filipino massaging technique called Hillot – I think that's what it was called. I let him do it only because then I got to massage his ankle. Payback's a bitch! When the bruising finally came out, it covered my arm shoulder to elbow. One of the guys from the gym took a photo of it, because he couldn't believe the size of the bruise. I know it sounds insane but we laughed about it; it looked so bad that it was funny. Hillot requires you to push out the swelling and get the bruising to the surface using a stick. Does it hurt? I can't even explain the pain! But does it work? Yes! In actual fact, the recovery is quite fast. My instructor taught me the basics, but I would still like to learn a lot more.

Sometimes in life you only get that one opportunity to show the world what you are made of. More importantly, you show yourself. The competition in New Zealand was my opportunity.

Stick fighting is a very intense sport because you're hitting for a minute non-stop, wearing four kilos of armour plus your sweat. The way this tournament was run, we were fighting every five to ten minutes, which didn't leave much time for recovery. We always had to be ready, because you didn't know when they were going to call your name out. The rush was unbelievable! There were eight fights going on at the same time. If we weren't there ready to fight, we were automatically disqualified, no second chances.

I can't remember how many fights I had, but I know they were all of high quality and all of them were hard, especially when I had to fight one of the toughest women I have ever had the pleasure of knowing. We went four rounds, when normally it's three, because they found it very hard to pick a winner. But I won the first competition and my first ever gold medal. I was really hoping to win a second, especially because it involved the double stick, which was my favourite. Once again we went four rounds, but this time I got silver instead.

The most frustrating thing about the tournament was the referee. He was not of this world, getting confused with who was wearing what. At one stage, he said I'd won and then changed his mind. Can you imagine being told you won, then a few minutes later you're being told, 'Sorry, I made a mistake'? No doubt it happens in other sports, but when you are the competitor, you want to kill the referee. However, once the fights were over, I had some perspective. I had a gold and a silver. All my hard work had paid off.

33

The big trip 2008–2009 – time for some space

Something I always wanted to do was combine training and travel, so at the end of 2008, that's exactly what I did. We first travelled to the Philippines; by we, I mean my instructor and a couple of other martial artists. The Philippines is not a place you would want to travel to on your own, unless you know the people. Lucky for us, we knew Cebu people.

We trained every day for four hours a day, two in the morning and two in the evening. I learned so much and made a lot of friends. The people there are so different. Life is very different. They don't have the opportunities we do and yet they accept the situation and remain at peace with it. I didn't ever see them sad; they were always happy and willing to help. Even though I was only there for eight days, it felt longer.

My next destination was America. I stayed there for four weeks, predominantly living in California, travelling between Malibu and Cornell. Due to the distance and the way LA is set up, I had to hire a car, though had I remembered that most places have public transport, I would have much preferred that. In any case, I didn't imagine I'd be driving minutes after landing in LA. Oh, my God, I couldn't believe it! I picked up the car, which of course was left-hand steering, and there I was driving down the right-hand side of the road. All I remember thinking was, please God, don't let me die, not on my first day here.

During my time there, I taught and participated in classes with other students. It was an amazing experience to exchange knowledge and skills and to see how other martial artists trained.

I also trained at one of the best known martial arts gyms in Los Angeles, the House of Champions. Its reputation precedes it! It attracts people from all walks of life – from people walking in off the street, to celebrities, be it on TV or on the field. One of the differences, compared to the martial arts gyms here in Australia, was the way the higher-ranked students were addressed. Whereas in Australia, you are addressed by your rank, in House of Champions or by American Martial Art standards, and unless you were a Master or Grand Master, you were addressed as Mr, Mrs, Ms or Miss followed by your surname.

I was also offered a job while I was there, but due to Wall Street crashing and visas costing the gods' earth, it wasn't meant to be. But the experience of training with such high-calibre instructors was enough for me.

After spending about a month in America, my next destination was New Zealand, specifically Christchurch. That's where I got to learn the art of wing chun which, according to the Oxford dictionary, is 'a simplified form of kung fu used as a system of self-defence'. Unlike other martial arts, where you either use weapons or your hands, it involves bringing together the combined strength of the mind and body.

At the time of my arrival, I was days away from celebrating New Year and, thanks to the instructor and his family, I didn't have to spend it alone. It was nice to spend it in a different part of the world where there was so much beauty and such good people. I couldn't have asked for a better New Year.

In addition to the training there was also a lot of sightseeing, some of which I did on my own. The heart of Christchurch is shaped very much like Adelaide, a square, so it was easy to find your way around, especially on foot. It had some amazing gardens and interesting things to look at, and that was only a small part of it. I would love to go again. Unfortunately, I only got to spend a week there but was invited to go back for a visit and for possible employment. The instructor and some of the students were very accommodating – another inspiring experience.

Last but definitely not least was the week I spent training and sleeping at the gym in Wollongong. The training was hard, but not as brutal as I was accustomed to, which was a nice change.

The experience of living and training overseas gave me a new found confidence that I'd never had before. I'd always wanted to have my own business, but until I came back from the big trip, I'd been too scared to take the risk. There was no reason I couldn't do it as I had no responsibilities at the time, other than the rental property that I now live in. It was just fear that stopped me.

So what did I learn overseas? I learned that I did want to take the risk. If all those other people could do it, then why couldn't I? It was always something my instructor tried to convince me to do. I wasn't ready before, but now I was. There is never a right time to take a risk. You just have to do it and even if the risk doesn't pay off, at least you tried. It's the same as seeking help. It took me a long time – my biggest regret – to build up the courage to go to a psychologist, but at least I did it. Everything has its time and place and the time was now.

The first decision I made was that I had to move out of home. I had been living with my sister for ten years and it was time for us to go our separate ways. In September 2009, I moved into a home of my own. Now I had my own home and my own business and some very good friends. For the first time ever, I was feeling very much in control of my own life.

I made another new friend that year, when I became friends with Ana. My recollection of meeting her for the first time is quite vague. She had been coming to the gym for about a year, but I hadn't noticed her at first. When I saw her there with a group of friends, I suggested that if they wanted to learn how to box, I would teach them. Apparently, some of them didn't want to get into the ring with me; they were scared that I'd hurt them. Lucky for me, Ana didn't listen to them. We decided that midday Saturday was a good time to meet. The first few times, two or three turned up, but gradually there was only the one, Ana! She was determined to learn and I was happy to teach her. She was relentless and could throw some really good punches. The funny part was that every time my instructor saw us spar, it was always 'Vickie, don't go hard.' As if I would!

34

The highs and the blows – a glutton for punishment!

It was Friday morning, a week before our trip to Wollongong. My instructor suggested we get in the ring for a little light sparring. As I discovered in that particular session, it doesn't take power to break something, but precision. The first couple of rounds were okay, but in the third round, my nose was hit and started to bleed. Every time I tried to clean it up, he would hit me again and the bleeding would start all over again. This issue was solved by the fourth round, when we heard a little crack. We weren't sure if it was broken, because it's hard to identify a broken nose. Well, that's until you see your eyes and nose get all puffy and swollen. Then we realised it was broken but we didn't know how badly. I remember saying to him, 'Can't you fix it and then we can keep going?' I only had one week for my nose to recover, before it was punished once again.

One week had passed and we were on our way to Wollongong for an in-house tournament. That's as close as you get to a real fight. I was pumped; even my instructor saw a change, telling me, 'The penny has dropped.' Unfortunately, because of my age I was never going to see another amateur fight unless I went professional, entered the Masters, or they included a thirty-five and over division. So this was basically it for now. In previous fights, I had suffered what felt like anxiety, but it was only this year that it had been identified by my psychologist as performance anxiety.

On the night of the fight, I drew the short straw, as in I was the last to fight. Everyone else from the gym had either won or drawn, which meant I had to do the same – no pressure! My instructor told me to start warming up and then it began.

I felt like I was having out of body experience. I could see, hear and was present, but in my head I was gone. I used to suffer panic attacks when I first started training but I hadn't had one for years, well, not until 2008, when it reared its ugly head again! I knew I was gone, but I wasn't sure what to do to make it go away. It wasn't about getting hit, especially after training with my instructor. His hits were real. I felt like I was running out of time. Maybe if I had got my instructor to hit me a few times, it could have made a difference, but there were only a few minutes left before show time. This was my last fight. I just had to win.

I entered the ring through the ropes. My heart was beating out of my chest. I didn't know how to control the sweaty palms and the sick feeling. I'd known something like this was going to happen. I had actually gone to see my psychologist but he convinced me I was fine. Boy, was he wrong! The bell rang and round one began. My whole body was in slow motion. I didn't even get time to throw a punch. My opponent had already thrown what felt like a million. She was bigger than me, but that was no excuse.

By that stage, there was more blood coming out of my nose than a dripping tap. After being broken only the week before, it hadn't exactly healed. We all knew she was going to go after the nose. I just didn't expect it to happen so quickly. It hurt like hell but that wasn't going to stop me. Round one was over and there were two more to go. What was I going to do?

My instructor could see I was struggling, so he figured reverse psychology might work. 'So you want to retire? Maybe you should retire after this fight.'

His words didn't motivate me; they actually had the opposite effect. I started to believe it. By the end of round one, I'd convinced myself I'd lost. The mind is an amazing thing; it can either make you or break you. For me, it was the latter and I ended up losing.

Of course it's polite to tell a fighter that they did a good job. That's what everyone did. 'You did a great a job' and 'Well done', but I knew the truth. I couldn't get out of there quick enough. I was devastated! I had let myself down. What would people say? How could I lose a third fight? I found the closest toilet and began to cry, and they weren't just little tears. I was sobbing like someone had died. Although I'd done well in stick fighting, I had yet to win a boxing match.

I was so disappointed after my loss in Wollongong that my instructor tried to cheer me up. No matter the losses, I just kept coming back. He had seen me through every fight and through every loss. He never gave up on the belief that one day I would eventually win.

It was around that time that I made another new friend, Theodora. We too became friends through training. A Greek import, Theodora came to Australia eleven years earlier to marry her Greek/Australian husband. They had two small children. Her husband was my accountant. He knew I was a personal trainer and the rest is history. Theodora and I became friends instantly. She was just a little shorter than me, petite, but can become a foot taller when wearing high heels! Theodora has blonde hair and a great accent but she also excels in the English language. She, too, is one of my biggest supporters, as I am hers. She always looks immaculate, even when we train – who does that? She is very ambitious and career-driven. She writes for a Greek newspaper and has her own radio slot. Theodora is one of those people who will do anything for you, especially if you're having a bad day.

35

Here we go again! – October 2010

In October 2010, I was finally ready to box again. There was another fight coming up in Wollongong.

So how does one prepare for a fight? I've experienced this a few times and the only word that comes to mind is discipline. It basically comes down to how much you want it. The preparation is the springboard to the fight. As my instructor says, the training is where it begins, and how you train will reflect in how you fight.

I'm not sure how other fighters prepare, but my preparation begins as soon as I agree to fight. I had exactly four weeks to prepare for this one. As soon as I agree, it's like the brain and body goes into fight mode, like they know what they have to do. It's the whole thing, the mind, the body, the training and, of course, the food. The hardest thing I've found when preparing for a fight is to maintain my weight. However, with experience under my belt, this time was possibly the easiest. I'm guessing it had a lot to do with the emotional release I experienced during those four weeks.

I managed to drop just over four kilograms in that month, but not without a few hiccups. Going out for dinner is difficult enough without having restrictions but, as I say to my clients, it's not like it's going to be your last dinner. Granted I was a little less disciplined when I went out for dinner, but I knew my body well enough that I could counteract the extra weight. It all comes down to portions and the method only works through experience.

The next setback was two weeks before the fight when I went to visit my parents. They were unaware that I was planning to fight again. By not telling them, I avoided the whole 'I thought you were going to stop', 'When are you going to fix your nose?' and 'You should be trying to find a husband, not boxing.' The list goes on and on, mostly from my mum, but no doubt my mum wouldn't be the only one saying it.

Therefore, to avoid all that, I sacrificed the weight loss and ate whatever they put in front of me, especially when it was my favourite dish: pasticcio. They also thought that I'd lost too much weight and needed to eat more, so I succumbed to the constant hammering and ate. Two steps forward, one step back – that became my life in those few weeks.

The next thing was the fitness. Not only do you have to be physically fit but, most importantly, mentally fit. First of all you must do as much sparring as you can. Sparring is actually getting in the ring and fighting against anyone and everyone. That's the way you simulate a real boxing bout. The rounds, the time, and the hitting are as real as you can get. The only difference is that you're not there to hurt the person. The sparring is about learning to get hit, what it feels like, how to counter, how to move, how to block, improving the fitness. It encompasses all the elements necessary to fight.

I would try and get in at least two to three times a week for sparring, averaging ten to twelve rounds a session. The rounds also depended on the intensity. When you only have four weeks to prepare, you try and get in as much sparring as possible. The sparring could vary. Because this particular fight was points-based, it was all about speed. I would go in on Monday, Tuesday and Thursday nights at 5 p.m. to do a few rounds and then participate in the class. Saturday was a normal sparring day, so I definitely had to be there then.

This was not my regime for the full four weeks. I was also trying to get assignments out for university, so it only occurred three out of the four weeks.

In those weeks leading up to the fight, when I was able to devote a lot of my time to it, I was probably averaging ten to twelve hours a week of hard training. I absolutely loved it. Don't get me wrong, though – it wasn't all smooth sailing. There were some difficult days, especially for a female pre-period. At that time you feel flat, emotional and can't be bothered. Thankfully, it was only for one or two days, but the preparation can be just as emotional as the fight itself. Some days I would come in pumped and raring to go, sparring really well and feeling really confident. Other days it was completely different – low self-esteem, not happy with my performance and just a crap session. The trick was just to accept it for what it was – a bad day – and then move on.

Unfortunately, for me it wasn't only the physical that I had to deal with; that bit was easy. It was all the emotional stuff that was going on. My biggest issue was the mind, so in our 7 a.m. sessions together, my instructor and I would do a lot of re-enacting. I explained to him that the problem was caused by performance anxiety. I couldn't focus on the fight, because there were too many other things going on in my head. What if I lost? What would people think? It just went on and on and so, by the time the fight started, I was already exhausted. My psychologist also defined it as a lack of external worth; basically, I didn't think I was good enough.

By understanding it better, I was also able to explain it better, so my instructor could understand how big a part it played in the ring – how the voices from outside the ring would interfere with my thoughts, thus suppressing my ability to fight. I'd become frozen. It was really good to be able to explain how I was feeling.

I spent a lot of time sparring with the boys. That was quite normal at the gym, any boxing gym really. The size, strength and physique all differed between the boys, which made them great for sparring, especially if you didn't know your opponent. Someone like Phil, who had a slender build and was fast with his punches, was great to spar with. We were about the same weight and could move around each other quite well.

On the other hand, Joe, who was six foot plus, solid, with a muscular build, was quite difficult to spar with: one, because of his long arms; two, his strength; and three, because one of his steps equalled three of mine. I still gave it a good crack, though.

Of course, I could never get out of sparring with my instructor. Much as the thought of sparring with him freaked me out, it was also very liberating. If I could withstand one of his punches, then anyone else would be a breeze.

As soon as I agreed to fight, my Monday and Friday 7 a.m. ju-jitsu sessions turned into boxing sessions. I remember asking whether we were going to do any more ju-jitsu during that month before the fight, and the response I got was 'You're going to sleep, eat and breathe boxing.' I'd had a feeling he was going to say something like that!

After all I had been through, I decided enough was enough. I was going to win at any cost. Why should I give away something I had worked so hard for?

36

Before the fight – an extract from my journal

The fight is coming up, and I have mixed feelings about it. The problem is this: I am not sure how I am supposed to be feeling.

As I was walking up those gym stairs yesterday, I was surprised by a sick feeling. My stomach felt like it was about to come out of my mouth. My heart was beating so loud and fast, I thought everyone could hear it. Granted the sick feeling only came back for a minute but it was still enough time to scare me.

I am really worried, but I guess it's better to have these feelings come now rather than during the fight. My psychologist is so confident that I will win; he wants me to call him and describe the medal. I'm not so sure!

This is all I can think about. I am trying to think positive, eliminating any negativity, which by the way includes people, but easier said than done. What if I lose again? What will people think? More importantly what will my friends think? I don't think I can handle another loss; it would be the end of me. I certainly wouldn't be able to show my face in the gym again.

I am feeling all kinds of emotions. On one hand I am confident that I can win, but then on the other hand I am scared, terrified at the prospect of losing. The hardest thing is the not knowing. How will I feel when I enter the gym? How will I feel when I enter the ring?

I took a deep breath, and hoped to God that this sick feeling I was normally accustomed to did not follow me from Adelaide to Wollongong like last year.

The fight was held at a boxing gym in Wollongong, and as the door was held open and we walked through to be greeted by the gym owners, I secretly feared the worst. What if it happened again? However, as I made my way through the small crowd, I felt OK. I was nervous, but I had stopped questioning my ability.

The gym was on one level. As we walked in, there were blue and red boxing bags hanging from the ceiling. Next to the bags was the boxing ring. The ropes that made up the ring were white, and there was a red pad and a blue pad on opposite sides of the ring. There was a positive feel to the place, a good atmosphere.

I had already dressed back at the hotel room, leaving nothing to chance. The breast protector was on underneath my shirt, which was black with our logo in white writing. The shorts were also on, elastic on the waist to avoid impact i.e. punches to the abdomen; with red writing against a white background that read 'Auspac'. Following a similar pattern, the name of the instructor was on each leg. On the reverse, the shorts had the name of the gym in white capitals with a red outline. Further down the leg on the left-hand side the word 'ACADEMY' was also displayed in capital letters.

I was still wearing my runners, not the correct footwear for boxing, but I would change into my boxing shoes before my bout. My hair had been braided the night before we left for Sydney, six little plaits, three on each side. I didn't want my hair to be an excuse for my performance. I even had my nails done. I think it's important to look the part, but also to try and look as feminine as possible.

An area was organised for us to put our stuff. All I had was my back pack, with all I needed inside, even my two cans of V-Drink. It's not the healthiest of drinks, but it was the one that made me feel good. It gave me that extra burst of energy, the feeling that I could train at a higher level. At the end of the day it probably made no difference to my fighting ability, but it was my equivalent to a safety blanket. Before putting my bag down I checked the board to see what number my fight was. The fights were written in a green marker. My name was spelt wrong, which really annoyed me. But I thought I'd look like a bit of a goose if I went and complained about such a detail, especially before the fight. I thought I might wait till after the fight, ha ha! I saw that my fight was number seven on the list. I was so happy, as waiting would've been the worst, and at least I would get to see Phil and Meg fight.

I thought my instructor might have had something to do with this. He probably thought I needed to get this out of my system as quickly as possible. Phil's fight was excellent. I can't remember every detail but he didn't even look like he was tired, and he looked controlled, seasoned in fact. A seasoned fighter is one who has had a lot of fights, but Phil, just like me, had had only four; he so wanted a win. You could see it through his style and technique. He approached his fight with such finesse that he had to win, and he did! I was really proud of him.

I managed to see some of Meg's fight but then it was my turn to get the Vaseline put on my face. My instructor was aiming to get the fighters done by order of fight, but I didn't want to wait. This gave us a final opportunity to go over all the stuff we had been talking about in the last few weeks. I told him I surrendered but he took it the wrong way. He thought I meant I had given up. In fact, quite the contrary; I was surrendering to everything that was to happen. I wanted to embrace the good and the bad and see where it took me. I no longer wanted to be that angry person with an attitude problem, who only showed one side of herself, the hard side.

I didn't want to live a life of regret, to have 'what ifs'. In order to move on, I had to forgive, and I came to the conclusion that boxing and relationships were never mutually exclusive; they were always linked.

I had to start warming up at the end of Meg's fight. It consisted of three rounds of skipping, shadow boxing and a few rounds on the focus mitts. Poor Phil was stuck with the job of warming me up. He apologised for being unfamiliar with the focus mitts. Punching them is much easier than holding them up for someone else.

At that point I felt like I was in control. I knew what I had to do and I did it. Shadow boxing is all about loosening up and practising your moves, ideally in front of a mirror. Quite the opposite to a normal gym, where looking in a mirror is considered vain and self-centred, but people do it anyway. There was some confusion about who was going to warm me up, as the Master was warming someone else up and my instructor was refereeing. In the past, this kind of scenario would have stressed me out. However, this time was different. I was in another headspace, and prepared for anything. It didn't feel like I'd warmed up for very long, perhaps it was the adrenalin; I just wanted to fight!

It was time. I decided not to change my shoes. I was ready to go. Whatever I should have or could have done would not change the outcome – whatever will be will be. Walking towards the ring, I felt confident and ready to show myself and the audience what I had. I could hear the well wishes of the other contenders and observers, but most importantly the words of wisdom that were coming from my team mates, and especially from my good friend Ana, who called me 'Champ'.

My instructor opened the ropes for me and gently I manoeuvred my body, placing one leg through so as not to fall over. Master D brought over the headgear. I liked the headgear because it covered my ears and head, but I could still see peripherally, unlike other headgear which covered my whole head, including my cheeks and jaw, and peripheral vision becomes difficult. The headgear was too big and covered my eyes, so my instructor asked Master D to find a smaller one. It was the perfect fit.

My opponent was a little taller than me, with short red hair. Her build was somewhat bigger than mine, and she apparently could throw an almighty punch. To her credit, she was six years older than me, which was quite inspirational. She was wearing a blue tank top with the Reflex logo on it, and shorts with the same logo. I hadn't seen her fight but, just by looking at her physique, I could see I would have a battle on my hands. My instructor had warned me that I needed to attack her straight away and not wait for her to come to me.

We each had our corner. The ring was bigger than the one in our gym. The floor was made of rubber and had quite a spring to it, whereas our ring floor was made of carpet. I was in the red corner, which was right of the entrance and she was in the blue corner. My instructor gave me some last minute advice: 'Just go straight in.'

Even though we were both orthodox fighters, which means we led with the left, our styles were very different. While they were taught to fight off the back leg, we were taught to fight off the front, which basically means we were taught to control the centre of the ring.

Seconds away, the referee introduced us both. We were asked to come into the centre of the ring. He held both of our hands and called out 'Fight.'

37

Six minutes – that's all it takes!

I came out guns blazing. I was firing with everything I had, just throwing punches. I couldn't tell what punches I was throwing, or how many. My aim was to make them connect.

I chased her around the ring, not stopping until the round was over. I felt my punches connecting, but I wasn't sure how many there were. I did as I was told and kept moving forward while punching. I didn't want to give my opponent any excuse to attack me. I don't remember too much of the round. It just felt like I was in trance, almost hypnotised. The only voices I could hear were my instructor's; the rest appeared to be muddled. That was a good sign. In the past I could hear everything everyone was saying, which distracted me from the fight. Moving forward, I managed to connect with every punch. I don't remember being tagged; in fact, it felt like I was the only one doing the hitting. The round felt short and I didn't feel too tired. I was out of breath, but easily recovered.

I felt good after the first round; I knew it was mine! The fact that I had two rounds to go didn't even enter my head. I think I was feeling a little cocky by the end of the first round. I couldn't wait to go back in and show her what I really had. In that one minute of rest, my instructor told me that now was the time to change my style and start circling her. That was something we had been working on leading up to the fight. I remember it took twelve rounds of boxing with my instructor on a Wednesday night to find my style, and this was it. Moving forward was not enough. I needed to confuse the opponent, which meant I needed to move left or right off the centre while hitting her.

It was all about timing. I had to make sure that when I was going to use it, it was going work. To be quite honest, I don't think my instructor was too fussed about whether it was going to work or not. I'm pretty sure just attempting it made him happy. I managed to pull it off, connecting her with a double right hook to the head, then a body shot. Unfortunately, it only happened the once.

She began to chase me. Not that I was backing down, but her punches began to connect, whereas mine were not. It was there as she stepped back I noticed my blood on her gloves, specks on the white parts of her gloves, clearly not hers. But you have to expect a little blood. Seeing my blood on someone else's gloves was nothing new to me. The novelty had long worn off and I had become quite accustomed to it. The sight of blood doesn't bother me. Nor can you feel the hit even when you do see the blood; it becomes part of the process. Nonetheless, while you're impressed that the opponent has drawn blood, you would still like the opportunity to fight back, perhaps draw some blood yourself, or create a little pain for them.

At that point I could hear my instructor saying, 'Your punches aren't hitting her.' Even before he told me that my opponent and I had one point each, I knew she had the round, but I wasn't worried. I knew I still had one round to go. I was confident that I could do it, not necessarily win, but do well. The only advice my instructor gave me was to throw any punch, and not stop until the round was over.

We met in the centre of the ring to begin the third and final round, touched gloves and began to fight. I wanted the win so much. I felt I had worked really hard and, to be quite honest I believed I deserved it. I thought, if anyone's going down, she is.

We were throwing punches, trying to outdo each other, trying to make the other tired, and trying to make the other give up. But I wouldn't give up. Tired wasn't even in my vocabulary, and I doubt very much that it was in hers.

This time it was not one-sided. I gave, but not without receiving. It's like Christmas! Before you enter the ring you have all these illusions, or should I say delusions, of what punches and combinations you're going to throw. It soon becomes apparent that the only punches you're going to throw are straights, and if you're lucky you might actually throw more than one. Thankfully, I was not under such an illusion. My biggest issue had nothing to do with the boxing; it was all about the mind. But now all I wanted to do was win. I didn't really know what the punches were, as long as they were connecting. Some did, some didn't.

At the last stages of the fight, she had the upper hand and was pushing me towards the ropes. I was still hitting, but then something happened. I slipped and fell onto my knees. I wasn't sure how much time I had left, or how I got to the ground. All I knew was I had to get up and keep fighting. My instructor thought we had more time, so he was yelling to get up and get back in there. The fall did cause a slight disappointment, but it didn't last long. I quickly realised there was no reason to be disappointed. I had fought well so, win or lose, I should be happy. As I proceeded to get up and continue to fight, the round ended. Now it was in the hands of the gods; whatever happens, happens – *C'est la vie*.

I went back to my corner. My instructor wiped my nose, cleaned up the blood and took off the headgear. My hair all messed up, nose looking a little worse for wear, I went back to the centre of the ring.

I had a conversation with myself in those last ten seconds of the fight, explaining to myself that it was OK; it didn't matter if I lost, I fought a good fight. The judges, sitting on opposite sides of the ring and holding red and blue sticks representing the fighters, had made their decision. Was it me or was it her? Did I say a little prayer? Yes. Did I what! Seconds felt like hours. I was anxious. How could you not be? It all came down to six minutes. As my instructor always said, 'If it's gonna be, it's up to me.'

The winner is identified when the referee raises their hand. Mine was raised; clearly I was the winner, but was I? Before jumping up and down and making my thank you speech, I thought I'd better check to see if my opponent's hand was also raised also. No! Could it be possible? I won! No fucken way! I couldn't believe we had done it. All that hard work had finally paid off! I was shocked, mentally exhausted and so very happy.

38

It only took eleven years – amen!

I was ecstatic because there was finally relief for both my instructor and me. Even though he told me he didn't care if I won or lost, it was how I fought that mattered. While I appreciated the gesture, it was obvious he was elated with my win. As a trainer, you have to wonder what happens if your fighters can't win at least one fight. Thankfully, he no longer had to worry. He told me, 'I knew you could do it.' I was also really glad that my friend Ana was there to support me and be part of the win. I dedicated the win to my instructor and friend. I know it sounds cheesy but it's important to acknowledge people, especially people who have helped you.

We all won. For a lot of the fighters, it was their first time competing but they did a sensational job and they made me feel proud. Was it the gym itself, or the instructor? I'll let you decide!

When we went back to our rooms, we were called into the common room for a little meeting, more like a thank you to our instructor for all his hard work. What I didn't see coming was his appreciation of us and of what we had achieved. He went round the room, mentioning each and every one of us, how well we had fought and how we hadn't given up. When he got to the third or fourth fighter, I realised he was going to talk about me last, and I hate being the centre of attention. However, what he had to say brought a tear to my eye; it was quite emotional. To cut a long story short, he called me an unsung hero, who never asked for anything, just trained hard and never complained, and remained humble. He said I could be an inspiration to the other fighters! How could I not want to cry? I held it together, though, just. So, as you can, see this was not just another boxing gym, with just another instructor; it was so much more.

This is the man who inspired me to become a personal trainer, to play a part in someone else's life and help them make a difference within. It was not the first time he had said that, and no doubt won't be the last. He had this amazing ability to make people believe they can achieve anything, and finally I believed I could.

His speeches were directed not only to the fighter; he also spoke about my friend Ana who, if she hadn't been pregnant, would have competed and won. Until the last week leading to the fights, I still felt like I needed to repay her in some way, but then I realised, this is what friendship is all about. To have someone believe in you makes all the difference because eventually you start believing in yourself. Once the result was in, I went over to my opponent and congratulated her. I also went to her corner and congratulated the coaches.

While the fight under normal conditions was small, the win was big. As I got out of the ring and was walking towards our area, my instructor came up to me gave me a kiss and hug and said, 'I'm proud of you, kid.'

It was quite emotional for me. I was still quite numb so I lay down on the nice, springy, soft mat, to think, to reflect, to take in what had just happened.

It was about an hour later when I started to send out a few hundred text messages. The first two went to my brother and sister; the next to my friends, and finally to my clients. The messages coming back were 'Congratulations!', 'So proud of you!' One came back with 'Won what?' and the funniest was 'So you finally got laid' – that was from my cousin. The responses were overwhelming, but that's what put this particular gym above the rest. The camaraderie was amazing. Much as we make fun of each other, or unintentionally hurt each other in the ring, we were family.

My clients were also very happy with my win, a few providing me with champagne and wine. While a nice gesture, I think it was more of a bribe, because they didn't know what to expect when I got back. Some thought I'd work them harder if I won; others thought I'd work them harder if I lost – neither a good choice in their eyes. Lucky for them I came back with a smile on my face, therefore giving them what they deserved. You work it out!

What does it feel like to win a boxing match? It took almost eleven years but finally I knew! The feeling is surreal. In fact, in the last ten seconds of the round, I actually thought I had lost, but that was okay, because I was happy with the way I had fought.

39

Working with kids – a change of priority

Having kids is not something I ever considered, and if someone had told me I would change my mind about it, I would never have believed them. But that started to change when my niece was born and even more so after the friendship I had with Melissa.

Once I discovered how much I liked kids, I started doing the out of school hours program, which involved taking kids through an hour of sporting activities after their normal school hours. Thinking that the task would be an easy one, I decided to take on three schools. It only took the first day to discover how sadly mistaken I was. It was one of the hardest things I had ever done. I was supposed to be there to teach them something, but instead they taught me.

One of the first schools I went to was located in a low socio-economic region, where volunteers were hard to find. At first glance, the children did appear to be difficult to deal with. As I got to know them, it was obvious that their rebellion was not something they were born with, but something they had developed over time. Their so-called bad attitude was simply a defence mechanism.

I made a connection with one of the children; our love for drawing was the link. I decided on the last day I would give him my old coloured pencils that I used to use for drawing. He was so happy to get them, but just as quickly as he got them, he was told to give them back. The children were not allowed to receive gifts! It was something I was not aware of, something I should have been told. He was devastated.

I was equally devastated and, to be quite honest, disappointed in the school system at the time. I had never seen a sadder face than the one that was put in front of me. Imagine putting a smile on an unhappy child's face and in that same instance taking it away. It broke my heart. I also think it was at this point that I decided I wanted to specialise in child psychology and also to train and work with kids.

It was a most exhausting seven weeks, but at the same time another milestone for me. Here was a person who had no time for kids – not that I disliked them; it was more that I couldn't tolerate them – but after that seven-week stint, my attitude changed. I became a softer person. I never thought I would have a soft spot for kids. I guess experiences like that opened my eyes to them. I felt like it was my job to be their protector, just as I felt about my young friend Melissa.

What I have discovered about children is that they can inspire you. They force you to be the best you can be. And I think our goal should be to make them proud of us not the other way round. The other thing I have learnt is to be less serious and have more fun with them. You can't train kids like you train adults – trust me, I tried!

After my experience at that particular school, I decided I needed a break. To be honest, I didn't think I was made for working with kids. It really took a toll on me. When I finally went back, I decided to take one school at a time, though it still didn't remove the challenge. Trying to keep thirty primary school kids focused was like trying to herd cats: it was impossible. Despite the challenges, they were still great to work with. They would ask me all kinds of questions. Are you married? Do you have a boyfriend? Do you have children? How old are you? Clearly they had no boundaries. The lack of boundaries also extended to their own parents. I heard all sorts of stories: my parents are divorced; my mum has a new boyfriend.

Other than training them in sports and martial arts, specifically self-defence (stranger danger), I really had no idea what I was doing. I just knew that I enjoyed it.

I trained children from different cultural backgrounds and family circumstances. The latter has become much more relevant as I continue as a mentor, working with kids with disabilities and learning difficulties, or those from broken homes.

40

When all is said and done – today

I gave up boxing in November 2011, just one year after winning my first big fight. Leaving the gym was like losing my best friend and it was one of the hardest things I had ever done. I had to learn to adjust to a life without training. There were no more 9.30 a.m. classes, no sparring Thursday or Saturday morning, and there were no more competitions. But it had to happen. We had grown apart. It had become a habit more than anything else. I was starting to take it for granted and, even more, starting to resent it. But what I also realised was that I couldn't find anything to replace it, because I tried!

I was OK to begin with. Working away kept me busy and between doing my own training at home and at the little twenty-four-hour gym nearby, it seemed to be enough. I discovered, however, that I really wasn't all right; you can't just stop doing something and be OK. I found myself mourning the loss of such an important part of my life. Training on my own in a 'normal' gym was just a mask, a cover. But, despite those feelings, I couldn't go back. I had two choices – learn to continue my life without it (and it wasn't like I didn't have other things to keep me busy: my business, uni assignments, catching up with friends) or be miserable. I chose the first.

I continued with my uni studies, achieving my Bachelor of Arts degree in 2013 and my Graduate Diploma in Counselling and Psychotherapy in 2014, all the while still running my own business in between. In 2016, I moved to Melbourne and finished my Masters in Counselling and Psychotherapy.

In addition to the out of school hours program, I also began volunteering as a mentor at a local primary school. The children I dealt with had a range of difficulties, from autism to social issues. It really challenged me, but it also had a profound effect on me, because even though I knew I wanted to work with kids, it was about more than that: it was about making a difference. I found that most kids responded to me quite well. Even though I had a tough exterior, they could see straight through me, and don't kids make the best judges of character?

I found training children challenging, but it also puts things into perspective. That's why I continue to do it today. I love it, not only because I get to learn from the children I'm mentoring, but because they also learn from me. It's a great responsibility and an absolute privilege.

They say, 'If you love what you do, you don't work a day in your life.' Some clients can be extremely challenging – to the point of my wanting to poke my eye out with a fork – because they don't see the potential I see. Sometimes they don't appreciate their own worth. They seem to feel they're not good enough and don't deserve the best. But it's very rewarding when the switch clicks. I never tire of seeing what happens when they get that spark, and they realise they can do it.

Some of my clients are so impressive, the way they overcome the odds to find their inner strength. One of my clients, a sixty-five-year old man who has had a quadruple bypass, trains like a demon and never gives up.

While some friendships have changed and people have moved on, I'm still blessed with the small group I have. I'm no longer paranoid about who hasn't contacted me, manifesting all kinds of scenarios in my head, making it more about me than them. Rather, I'm more appreciative of the time I get to spend time with them when we do catch up.

There is also a confidence that they're not going anywhere and that it's OK to depend on them if I have to. And I think that comes from the fact that I have somehow developed or discovered a self-worth, that my own goals are just as important as theirs.

Having time off from study in 2015 meant that I could concentrate on other things, such as my mentoring, volunteer work and getting back to boxing – which I never thought I would do. I missed it and eventually had to come back to it. But it's different now. It's not about impressing other people; it's not about the competition. It's about doing it for myself. Boxing awakens something in me, more so now, because even I recognise my own potential. It's something I know I do well and it's something I love. Boxing brings out my inner strength.

41

Lessons I have learnt – two steps forward, one step back

I have learnt so many lessons from my experiences as a boxer, the main one being to look inside myself in hard times and find the boxer within. I have learnt to fight to be the best version of myself that I can be.

I have found myself no longer obsessing about being on my own, and rather focusing on just being happy. It's like something has shifted. Not to say that every day is going to be a good day, and I may default, but I'm still choosing to be happy. I'm focusing more on myself, the plans I have and the new chapter that begins in 2018.

Other lessons I have learnt are:

I will never give up.
I create my own opportunities.
I do what makes me happy.
I am resilient.
I believe that eventually we find our passion or it finds us.
What I do isn't who I am. I won't let anything define me.
Anything is possible, but it depends on how much you want it.
Self worth is vital, without it you have nothing.
I can be fearless with my heart.
I have nothing to prove to anyone but myself.

This has been my story, my experiences, my therapy, my way of helping myself and hopefully others, if they want it. My intention was never to downplay other people's stories or issues. This is simply my way of describing how boxing helped me overcome so many difficulties and how it's helped me deal with new challenges.

My last piece of advice is to learn to keep the faith, be patient, listen, consider others' thoughts and feelings, but most importantly to enjoy the ride no matter how scary it is. So go be fearless!

Thanks

To my friend Helen Wright, thank you for giving me the idea in the first place.

To Catherine Wait, thank you for your patience, time and making me love the English language again.

To Stephanie McNally née Hester, thank you for making me write forty pages and pitching the idea at the Salisbury Writing Festival. You are one in a million, always putting others first, but now it's your time to shine.

To Professor Nicholas Jose, thank you for taking me under your wing, not only as my professor but also as a supervisor. Your faith that this book could be more than just a book just shows the kind of belief you have in your students.

To my family, thank you for your support, and especially to my siblings Matina, Sam and my sis-in-law Gina for believing in my abilities, even when I didn't. You guys rock!

To the friends who let me put them in the book, your friendship has taught me so much and I am forever grateful.

To Vicki Mavrakis, what can I say? Eleven years of friendship, my person, Christina Yang to my Meredith Grey, you taught me more about strength and resilience than anyone else ever could.

To Rodin Genoff and Susan Petiffer, thank you for your many years of friendship and making me believe that the sky's the limit.

To Sandy Litt, for helping me through some of these troubled times. I am no longer an emotional time bomb.

To my niece Kayla, who would kill me if I didn't mention her. Even though I don't get to see you and your brother Tom too often, your enthusiasm, energy and perspective on how the world should work make me proud to be your aunty and I thank you.

To Sandra Lindemann, thank you for your time, patience and direction and letting me be part of the editing process.

To Jack Centofanti, thank you for introducing me to the world of martial arts and for your patience, especially because of the injuries I almost caused you.

To the instructor who made this journey more than I could've ever imagined. Although our lives have taken different paths, thank you for pushing me to do my absolute best.

To Con and Theodora Maios, thank you for your friendship and support over the years and for trusting me with your kids while you were training.

To my Adelaide and Melbourne friends, thank you for your friendship and support.

To my martial arts friends, thank you for making the journey an enjoyable one and for the life long memories.

To my cousin Vicky Karamanis, thank you for your encouragement, support and for helping me with the book cover. I miss our Wednesday night catch-ups!

To my PT clients, who also became friends, thank you for sharing your stories with me. I am humbled.

To Cathy Beech, thank you for being the best teacher any kid could ask for. Your dedication to the profession and your students has always been inspiring.

To Paul Bovolos, thank you for creativity and making me look so good.

To Zara Jones, thank you so much for making me look and feel fabulous. You turned the ordinary into the extraordinary.

To the House of Champions for having me, and to all the other martial arts instructors who let me train with you when I was overseas.

To Cacoy Doces Pares Eskrima.

To Ginninderra Press, thank you for agreeing to publish my book. You have made a dream come true.

And last but not least to the boy who started me on this journey: if it hadn't been for you, the second part of this book might have never happened, so thank you!

www.ingramcontent.com/pod-product-compliance
Lightning Source LLC
Chambersburg PA
CBHW030909080526
44589CB00010B/224